In Words & Pictures

Thomasville

in the Nineteen Twenties

By Wint Capel

CapeCorp Press

Chapel Hill, North Carolina
1999

To Bob Rapp — Best Wishes, Wint Capel 25 Aug 99

(c) 1999 by Wint Capel

All rights reserved. No part of this book may be reproduced in any form or by any electronic means, including information storage and retrieval systems, without permission in writing from the author, except by a reviewer, who may quote brief passages in a review.

Published by CapeCorp Press in association with Marblehead Publishing, Raleigh, N. C.

Printed in the United States of America

To communicate with the author, write:

>Wint Capel
>1511 Hatch Road
>Chapel Hill, N. C. 27516

Library of Congress Catalog Card Number: 99-61134

ISBN 0-943335-14-0

Introduction

Before telephones became commonplace in Thomasville, the most dependable and economical way to communicate over any distance at all was via the federal government's U. S. postal service. And for a long time afterward Thomasville residents with a need to transmit a message or information efficiently found that a letter entrusted to the U. S. mails remained the cheapest, usually the most practical manner in which to get it done.

A letter or, yes, a post card.

Surely cheap is the right word for the cost of sending a card. For years it required only a one-cent stamp, or, cards imprinted with a one-cent stamp and available at any post office could be purchased for only a penny. For almost a hundred years, in fact, they were simply and for the best of reasons known as penny post cards.

The cost was a penny from the time the postal service first put cards on sale in 1873, or four years after this form of communicating was dreamed up in Austria. It did not change until 1952, except briefly during World War I, when raised to two cents. For practically always, a card, to qualify for post card rates, has had to be no more than 3 1/2 inches wide and no more than 6 inches long. Not until 1898 did the postal service provide for accepting at the one-cent rate the so-called private mailing post card, that is, those privately produced and to which an adhesive U. S. stamp had been affixed.

From the beginning cards were found to be handy, but became even more popular after the onset of the practice of illustrating one side appealingly, making them, indeed, picture post cards. Credit for this refinement, dating back to about 1890, goes to the Europeans as well. Not long after that date -- and before the advent of the Kodak box camera -- a Thomasville resident vacationing at Carolina Beach could mail home a photo of people splashing merrily in the sun-drenched surf there, a picture post card no less, one that had been purchased for a nickel or a dime at a nearby drug store or hotel. Most likely the message on the side opposite the photo read "Wish you were here."

Usefulness of all kinds of mail increased markedly after Congress made Rural Free Delivery (RFD) a part of the postal service in 1902. The farmer's isolation ended. It became possible for him to receive an issue of the local newspaper within a day after it had been printed. He welcomed the mail carrier's arrival with a Sears & Roebuck catalog. Advertisements began to fill up his mailbox, along with more letters and cards. One of the latter reproduced in this book was sent from Thomasville to the resident of a Thomasville RFD route who was probably a farmer. It could have reached its destination no later than one day after it had been mailed. The message thereon: "Dear Papa, when you come tomorrow please bring two bushels of apples."

Rural Free Delivery was truly a break-through. It touched off a good roads movement and paved the way for parcel post.

Cards bearing Thomasville illustrations date back at least until 1907, which is roughly the start of a period when not just card-sending but card-collecting as well reached out and captured the public's fancy. It is estimated more than a billion cards were manufactured during this time, a great many of which came from Germany, where sometimes they were colored by hand. That country was a chief source up until about 1914, or until World War I interrupted commerce between Germany and this country.

Sending and collecting have remained popular, of course. Not with the intensity and fervor of 75 to 80 years ago, but an astonishing variety of cards, some little works of art, are on sale at many places. And great numbers from the past are either in old trunks or still in circulation. Those deemed to be collectibles continue to increase in value, occasionally at incredible rates. In 1998 one dated 1912 sold at public auction for $24,150. It survived the sinking of the *Titanic*. A passenger had it in her pocket to be mailed when she became one of the fortunate few who made it to safety in a lifeboat.

On the earliest Thomasville cards are the credit lines of J. M. Morris & Son, a general merchandise business in The Chair Town. Undoubtedly this firm engaged a professional to photograph local structures of interest and then sent his prints if not his negatives to some publisher in Germany with an order to have them converted into post cards. Not long afterward, the products of this process would have been on sale and in stock at the Morris store.

In step with what Morris had going was Charles R. Thomas,

grandson of the founder of Thomasville (John Warwick Thomas) and proprietor of a popular downtown fixture in Thomasville, Thomas Drug Store. It appears he delved deeper, and for a longer period of time, into the card trade than Morris. Some of his that were made after World War I are marked "Made in Germany" and, judging by the logos on some, Thomas cards were being produced as late as 1929.

In fact, a majority of those reproduced in this book are the result of the enterprise of this drug store owner. More of his than anybody else's turn up in collections of the ones having Thomasville ties. At one time or another he had photos made of every eye-catching place, building and house in The Chair Town. Logos suggest that 1927 was his busiest time.

Additional evidence is a note in the Thomasville column of news appearing in a September 1927 issue of The (Lexington) Dispatch. "C. R. Thomas," it was reported, "now has on display at his store his magnificent assortment of post cards and the supply is all but inexhaustible and pictures many places of interest in the city, one of the important being the Baptist Orphanage. Several of the pretty residences of the city are in pictures, as are Main and Salem streets, also the big chair. Each one of the pictures has a tinge of blue sky at the top and gives it a setting natural, but not strained. Probably the demand for these cards will be constant and liberal."

Deltiology, from the Greek word meaning small writing tablet, is the study and the collecting of post cards. It is doubtful there exists a single bona fide deltiologist in Thomasville, but abroad nevertheless are quite a few individuals who either save or trade in cards, old and not so old, while gathering up or trafficking in antiques and other collectibles. Or have a few in family albums or attic trunks. From some of these it has been possible to borrow cards and have them copied for inclusion in this book. Without them, their cooperation, their generosity, and their desire to preserve Thomasville history, this volume could not have been.

But here it is, and what it tries to do has not been attempted before, to combine narrative and pictures to show what Thomasville must have been like during the volatile 1920s, when the town was growing rapidly, the standard of living rising, values changing. Little has been recorded about this fascinating decade, in part because there are no files now of Thomasville newspapers published prior to 1930. The most fertile field for research, the week-by-week accounting of occurrences that the newspapers could have provided, is missing. In addition, the few histories about Thomasville shed precious little light on what conditions were like and exactly what was taking place. This book then addresses the sizeable deficiency that has prevailed. By the use of words and pictures the author hopes he has filled in many of the gaps, and that he has done so in a manner to please the reader.

Most of the cards reproduced are from the Twenties. The rest are older, and have been included only because making a record of them might somehow add to the Thomasville store of what is historically significant. The accompanying narrative appeared in a somewhat different version in another book by the author, one entitled *Dethronement of Reason, The Travails of North Carolina's Murderous Dr. J. W. Peacock,* CapeCorp Press, Chapel Hill, N. C. 1998 (about the 1921 Thomasville calamity in which the doctor, in an ambush shooting, killed the town's police chief). Then it was a chapter with the heading "The Town of Thomasville." For the purpose of this book, it has been extensively rewritten and greatly expanded.

Wint Capel
Chapel Hill, N. C.
March 1999

This caricature of Charles R. Thomas appeared in the May 7, 1925, issue of Thomasville's *The Chairtown News,* one in a series of sketches by Cecil Webb of individuals well known in The Chair Town. Webb was associated with Thomasville Baptist Orphanage. Caption for this one of Thomas, with him sitting, noted "He seldom sits down. He believes in work and does a lot of it. He is a successful druggist, yet has time to grow the best and biggest garden in the city. His favorite pastime is making money, and his favorite sport is horseback-riding."

Acknowledgements

The financial support of two organizations in Thomasville has made possible the publication of this book, the T. Austin Finch Foundation and the Doak and Agnes Finch Foundation. The author expresses his gratitude to these two forces that for many years have continually and repeatedly committed their resources in a manner to greatly enrich the Thomasville community as a place to live, work and enjoy life.

The author also thanks those who have been willing to loan post cards for reproduction in this book, especially Clara Harris, Norman Saunders, Mike Connally, and the Hedricks -- Darrell, Hilda and Heather. Others were Cecil Hiatt, Margaret Honeycutt, Nat Walker and Ken Bowers. Due thanks, too, are Mary Hill, the Cecil Allen Custom Color Lab, and the Mills Home Museum for their assistance in locating and processing cards.

The encouragement and cooperation of the Thomasville Historical Preservation Association as well is gratefully acknowledged. This organization, the author trusts, will be a partner in and a benefactor of the marketing of this book in order that its members might succeed even more in their mission to preserve and promote an appreciation of Thomasville history.

LARGEST CHAIR IN THE WORLD. THOMASVILLE. N. C.

When towering over the two men (identity unknown) shown on this post card, produced by C. R. Thomas and issued in 1927, Thomasville's original Big Chair seems to be worthy of its title, "World's Largest." Measuring 13 feet 6 inches tall, it stood near The Square, symbolic of Thomasville's sizeable furniture industry, from 1922 until taken down in 1936. Long exposure to the weather made it unsightly. The present Big Chair, of concrete, was erected on the same site in 1951.

VIII

Thomasville Atingle

The dawn of the 1920s found Thomasville to be a bustling manufacturing center of between 5,000 and 6,000 souls. It was just as large and as productive as Lexington, the only other municipality in Davidson, a county situated in Central North Carolina.

Each town had sprung up astraddle the North Carolina Railroad, later the Southern Railway, then the Norfolk Southern. Their ventures into manufacturing were aided by good road connections as well as rail. A major highway that sliced through both downtowns went to Richmond in one direction and to Atlanta in the other.

The high level of business activity in Thomasville in the second decade of the century was a continuation of lively growth during the first. Back then, almost every year two or three new factories had appeared, practically all of which were quite small and produced plain, straightback wooden chairs. Their creations were only slightly less basic than the ones D. S. Westmoreland had been making in the factory he opened on Randolph Street in 1879. Westmoreland's (Thomasville Chair Factory) was the first chair plant in North Carolina and arguably the state's first true furniture manufacturing operation. A dozen of his hickory chairs, with spindle backs and three coats of varnish, sold for twelve bucks.

2

A conspicuous structure in Thomasville for years was the yellow, multi-storied building with green shutters pictured on this C. R. Thomas post card issued in 1927. The Thomasville Shooting Club acquired it in 1894 and used it until 1941 (it was razed soon thereafter). Individuals at the steps have been identified as (from left) Archie Primm, club manager; C. R. Thomas, drug store proprietor; and C. L. Harris, merchant. (This card and the one on the front of this book are the same.)

While perhaps not making them much better, Westmoreland's successors were making chairs faster. For several years in the early 1900s, Thomasville could boast its output was so great there was one to sit in for every man, woman and child in town.

(The output of soot and cinders was considerable, too -- from the coal-burning locomotives plying the tracks that split the town in halves and the factory smokestacks. Thomasville had them to thank for its dinginess.)

Before long the slogan "Chair Town of the South" had been adopted (Thomasville was closing in on Grand Rapids, Mich.) and in 1922, on the Town Square, there arose a statue, the town's first, a wooden dining room chair 13 feet tall. This curious reflection of an expanding furniture industry debuted as the largest chair in the world. Wags, or punsters, immediateley, and shamefully, labeled it the town's big asset.

The transition from town to city had been under way since 1910, or soon thereafter. In area, Thomasville grew from being one mile square to being 2 1/4 miles long and 1 1/2 miles wide. A slogan some switched to was "The Chair City: Seat of Diversified Industry." City status became undeniable after a bold step in 1915, a surge of progressiveness seldom seen before or since. The original charter was ripped up and the city manager form of local government embraced. Thomasville became only the third municipality in North Carolina to do this. Today, nearly every Tar Heel city has changed over and the governments of most counties now also have managers.

Diversification occurred with the emergence of two cotton mills; plants that made hosiery; makers of wooden veneers and panels needed in furniture-manufacturing; and a concrete products producer. Community leader J. W. Boyles's Thomasville Bottling Works, which turned out 50 cases of Coca-Colas and other soft drinks in his first year,

4

COMMONS, SHOWING SOUTHERN RAILWAY DEPOT, THOMASVILLE, N. C.

The photographer stood near where today a water fountain exists when around 1912 he put on film this view of the railway passenger depot and (at right) the freight depot. Main Street was still dirt. Back of the passenger station is the Mock Hotel. Most visible part of the freight depot is its office, today the restored railroad station on West Main. This card was published by R. G. Brooks 5 & 25c Store, Thomasville.

1907, was racking up more than 200 dozen cases by 1921, and also selling coal, ice, and ice cream. Amazon, one of the cotton or yarn mills, built a hundred houses -- a mill village, in fact -- and rented them to employees for 25 cents a room per week. The other yarn mill, Jewel, followed suit. It created a village of 65 "cottages." Chair factories also began to make bedroom suites and living room pieces. One of the owners of Thomasville Chair Co., Charles F. Finch, constructed 30 houses around 1912 and sold them to his employees at rates varying between $5 and $10 a month, or slightly more than rent.

The making of hosiery had been introduced in 1916 by W. Casper Pennington in a building on Taylor Street which soon became known as the home of Thomasville Hosiery Mills. Others set up knitting machines. Production and profits grew. Before long hosiery was, and remains, of course, a major player in Thomasville manufacturing. Ragan Knitting Co. was organized in 1918 and Maurice Mills in 1925. The output of wearing apparel received yet another boost with the organization of Carolina Underwear Co. in 1928.

Drummond's Pictorial Atlas of 1924 depicted Thomasville with 30 manufacturing businesses, two hardwares, three drug stores, two Five & Dimes, two wholesale houses, and 30 merchandise and grocery emporiums.

That year, 1924, was a time the womenfolk sang out hallelujah. Thomasville Family Laundry opened, providing an alternative to boiling the bedsheets in a big black pot in the backyard and hanging them out to dry on the trusty family clothesline. Hardly anyone had been responding to the invitation of a steam laundry in Charlotte, to put what was dirty on the train and for a small fee get it back all clean -- including dry-cleaned -- and neatly packaged.

6

This C. R. Thomas post card issued about 1910 looks from some distance, and across the Southern Railway tracks, at Thomasville's Town Square. On one corner is the Lambeth Building, erected in 1902. Its ground floor is occupied mainly by Thomasville Drug Store. Left of the building is the old John W. Thomas residence, a portion of which is visible.

Much earlier, in 1909, the Town Council passed an ordinance making it unlawful for local druggists to continue to dispense cocaine. But apparently that did not adversely affect an interchange evolving at the hands of Thomas J. Stanback, young manager of one of the local drug stores. Demand for a headache remedy he originated, a powder not known to need the pizazz of a narcotic, only increased. When he relocated in the Town of Spencer as a pharmacist in 1911, he began to sell his potions in little paper packets. Soon, as Stanback Headache Powders, these were selling briskly in many parts of the South. There has been no let-up. Today, a Stanback is one of the nation's most-in-demand treatments for a mal de tete.

Druggists often in those early times and even later were doctoring droves of people who didn't have the immediate benefit of a physician for some reason. "Doc, have you got anything for ... " is how consultations with them started out so often. One of Thomasville's most colorful individuals back then, a drug store fixture, was addressed also as Mr. (C. R.) Thomas, or as Charlie, and from time-to-time identified as "Charlie Red" if he was out of earshot. This redhead was owner of a store in the downtown area that sold a little bit of everything. At the beginning of each school year, students learned what books they would need, then went to Thomas Drug to buy them, that and any other school necessities. A grandson of the founder of Thomasville (John Warwick Thomas), "Charlie Red" not infrequently filled an order for castor oil, widely used, of course, to relieve an assortment of distresses. Believe it or not, he could make a dose of the awful stuff taste fairly good, people said. According to perhaps the most oft-repeated "Charlie Red" anecdote, he was standing early one evening at his soda fountain, Thomasville's first, when a little old lady approached and expressed her need for one of those castor oil concoctions he was famous for.

On the address side of this Thomasville post card is a 1912 postmark. The building shown was named the C. R. Thomas Block and had been erected by his father, Dr. R. W. Thomas. One of the tenants is C. R.'s Thomas Drug Store, established in 1899. The brick building, in the first block of West Main Street, also housed the Bank of Thomasville. A familiar downtown sight was the big Thomas Drug sign on the side of the building illustrated with mortar and pestle.

He indicated a readiness to accommodate. "Won't be but a minute or two." And, before disappearing into the back of the store where he usually compounded his essences of this and that, he served his customer a root beer to enjoy while she waited. He was gone what seemed a long time. Finally, the customer yelled out, "Ain't you finished yet? Where's my castor oil, anyway?" Charlie called back, "You already drunk it." The woman threw a fit. "You crazy old coot," she raged, "that was supposed to be for my sick husband." It's a good bet, however, that this tale was a well-worn skit on a vaudeville circuit somewhere before it turned up in Thomasville with yet another, a different, strictly local cast of characters.

Starting in the Spring and lasting well into the Fall, milltown life was made less dreary by baseball. The larger factories all sponsored teams made up of employees who had been hired only because of their knack for throwing, catching or hitting a baseball with outstanding results. Nothing drew a greater mass of noisy townspeople than a ball game. On the job, the player-employee, or semi-pro, was easy to spot. That was him there, the one sitting and day-dreaming in the open factory window while behind him his sweaty co-workers hustled about to keep the machinery producing profitably.

One of the industrial teams had as a player-manager for a while none other than Jesse Morgan (Rube) Eldridge, at the tail end of a remarkable career as a professional baseball pitcher. This product of Glenola, near High Point, had been ranked by many for several years as the most gifted baseball player in North Carolina. He could easily have been a big success in the majors, but, he would say, "I don't want to play anywhere I can't walk home." To sports writers he had a "million-dollar arm and a ten-cent head." Rube gave much of the credit for his incredible pitching prowess to his "needle-threadin' control," which, he

Salem Street was still a muddy passageway when the photo for this post card was made. The camera was pointed southward, toward the Town Square. Only horses and buggies were about. In April 1918 Thomasville issued bonds in the sum of $8,000 to finance a street-paving program that got under way soon thereafter.

claimed, he developed, as a youngster, by throwing acorns through the knotholes in a side of the barn back of his house. "The worst whuppin' I ever got," Rube would reminisce, "was the day my old man sent me out into the woods there at home with three smooth rocks and I come back with only two squirrels."

The favorite varsity sport for Thomasville high schoolers was, naturally, baseball. Football could be found gaining ground in some places but school Supt. J. N. Hauss outlawed it in Thomasville as a beastly activity. The school's first football game (an at-home 18-0 win over China Grove) did not take place until October 7, 1927, which was less than a year after Hauss departed to take another job (he returned a few years later). His leaving opened the way to year-around sports at the school, football in the Fall, basketball in the Winter and baseball in the Spring.

(Thomasville's first football coach was C. B. Eller, also a history teacher. His arriving to lead the school into a new sports experience came well into the Fall. At the first team practice Eller gave these instructions: "There isn't much time to learn the fine points of the game, so, just remember, anytime you see anybody standing up, knock him down." Eugene (Strawberry) Webb, son of druggist E. L. Webb, was unopposed for the position of quarterback. His qualifications: He was the only team member ever to have seen a college football game.)

While what little tennis being played apparently did not attain school sponsorship, it enjoyed high visibility. A tennis court, or ground, was laid out downtown, on a vacant lot next to Main Street Methodist Church, by, according to a newspaper, "some of our tennis boys and girls." As the paper reported in May 1917, "This is a good game of exercise and sport and no doubt but what it will be largely patronized by the younger set."

It appears that the Lambeth Building on this Thomasville post card is yet to be occupied. It was built on the Town Square in 1902. First to occupy the ground-floor corner was probably Thomasville Drug Store. In an extensive 1953 remodeling by a new owner, State Commercial Bank, the building acquired a third floor that afforded additional office spaces. Today, the building is still sturdy and fully utilized by a variety of business concerns.

The Twenties gave birth to the heroic era of American sports. The heroes most adored by sports fanatics were Babe Ruth of baseball, Jack Dempsey of boxing, Red Grange of football, Bill Tilden of tennis, and Bobby Jones of golf. More than any other, Ruth, Sultan of Swat, symbolized the love affair between the public and the famous athletes of the era. Fans forgave him for his riotous living as long as he was hitting homeruns. A preacher who became pastor of Thomasville's Grace Lutheran Church -- and presided over the funeral for Dr. J. W. Peacock's wife Pearle -- had a short-lived close relationship with Dempsey. It happened in 1923 while the Manassa Mauler was training in Asheville for the defense of his heavyweight title against Luis Firpo. While among those gathered to watch a Dempsey workout, the Rev. Charlie Patterson mindlessly and recklessly consented to take the place of a sparring partner who was tardy. The preacher, who had boxed some while in the Army, could brag later he never hit the canvas over the course of five grueling rounds with the champ but he lost one tooth and parts of two others. Dempsey's handlers were impressed. They returned the $2.50 that Patterson had spent on a ticket admitting him to the workout area.

There were all kinds of other heroes, of course, such as Charles A. Lindbergh. Some historians insist that the arrival of the age of air transportation was truly accepted only after the dramatic New York-to-Paris flight by Lucky Lindy in 1927. This first solo, nonstop crossing of the Atlantic earned for him instant celebrity. Afterward, he toured the United States in his monoplane, "The Spirit of St. Louis," to accept the adulation of thousands. He stopped in Greensboro October 14, 1927, then in heading for Winston-Salem later in the day for yet another hero's reception, he flew over several central North Carolina towns, including Thomasville, where school children were

14

The Cates Block in Thomasville was built in 1911 and was no more than a year or two old when the photograph for this post card was taken. Located on the east side of the first block of Salem Street, it housed Crutchfield Hardware (left) and The Burgin Co. The vacant space at right later became the home for a brief time of the U. S. Post Office. In the foreground is a town water pump. The Cates Block remains in use today.

massed in the school yard to wave to "The Lone Eagle" in case he were to pass their way. A newspaper noted that Lindbergh acknowledged what he saw in Thomasville. He "turned and serenaded the school children by circling the building and seemingly taking the children in his arms. He must possess a good heart."

Around 1920, or some 18 years after the Wright Brothers were the first to fly, airplanes went from being a curiosity to, some felt, being a nuisance. The trouble was, barnstormers kept showing up on Sundays. Many in the crowds they attracted were willing to cough up a dollar or two for the thrill of going aloft and buzzing about for 15 to 20 minutes. So eager to experience flying were they that Sunday school and worship service attendance began to suffer. The pastors, the newspaper and others complained about "Sunday air-riding" until the Thomasville City Council finally gave in and while in special session in September 1921 adopted an ordinance that warned henceforth "It is unlawful for any person, firm or corporation to operate a flying machine, airplane, or any like mechanical appliance which is driven through the air over the territory covered by the corporate limits of the City of Thomasville between the hours of 6 a.m. and 8 p.m. on the Sabbath Day. Any person violating this shall be subject to a fine of $25.00 for each offense."

Neither barnstorming nor blue laws, however, had anything to do with the stop made in Thomasville by two planes in November 1920. One was piloted by George William Haldeman of Lakeland, Fla., the other by Waldo S. Boyd of Maine. Haldeman had come to town to get married, Boyd to be his best man. Soon after they landed, a wedding ceremony took place at the home of Dr. J. W. Peacock, uncle of the bride, 20-year-old Virginia Lufsey, also a flying enthusiast. For some reason she preferred to say her wedding vows in Thomasville rather than her

16

In the close-up of Thomasville's Town Square on this 1927 C. R. Thomas post card it can be seen that drug stores dominate two corners, C. R. Thomas Drug at left in the Frank Lambeth Building and Harville Drug in the John Lambeth Building. Each store is blessed with awnings. The Thomas name is spread over one of these, and appears as well in the logo on this card, to show he produced it.

hometown of Lakeland. It was a fairly ordinary ceremony except that halfway through it the bridal couple left and stuffed themselves into Haldeman's plane. Close behind were best man Boyd and Dr. Peacock, who boarded Boyd's plane. Minutes later, the brace of airships was circling the bell tower of High Point's Wesley Memorial Methodist Church. First, the bells rang out Mendelssohn's wedding march, then the one from Lohengrin, after which the flying machines returned to Thomasville and the wedding ceremony picked up at the point it had been so unconventionally interrupted. It may have been the first time a bride had heard her wedding music come not from above but from below. From Thomasville the newlyweds took to the air, again in the groom's plane, and roared off to a honeymoon in Cuba, leaving the people in Thomasville to wonder what in the world had been going on.

Five months later, Dr. Peacock, one of Thomasville's four physicians and undoubtedly the most admired, found himself in deep trouble. A feud between him and a new chief of police culminated in a shooting on a busy Salem Street that left the lawman dead. The physician, possibly fearing the heavily armed J. E. Taylor was gunning for him, fired on the officer with a shotgun from a second-story office window and then descended and finished him off with a World War I souvenir, a 9mm German Luger. Peacock's career as a physician was over. After a trial, prison confinement, and an escape he wound up living in exile in California. A brilliant individual, he died there in 1928 in a mining accident.

The bitter, deadly Peacock-Taylor quarrel was fueled in part by the fault Peacock found with the chief's crusade against consumption of strong drink and gambling at cards. It was Prohibition during the Roaring Twenties and community morals were becoming less inviolate. It was like that everywhere. Drinking actually increased. Finding a

18

A portion of the Town Commons, studded with the originial Big Chair, is visible in the photo on this 1927 C. R. Thomas post card providing not only a full view of the Town Square but also a look at the town's principal railroad crossing. In addition, at far upper left, is the old John W. Thomas homeplace. This photo probably was made at the same time as the one on another card in this collection affording a close-up of the Town Square.

way to do it and not get caught was a game some played. The righteous wanted it all stopped but just as many in Thomasville thought the police chief was meddling beyond the call of duty and hoped he would be replaced.

Generally speaking, the level of meanness in Thomasville was low. The first bank robbery did not occur until 1967. Still, the community had found itself mourning the loss of police officers to foul play far more often than it would have liked. Including Chief Taylor, three had died after having been surprised with bursts of gunfire. That is, half of those slain up until the present day while acting in the line of duty were lost during the unpredictable, unprecedented 1920s. The other two were Officer Man Clodfelter, fatally wounded in 1920 while attempting to place under arrest two hobos at the Thomasville railroad depot, and Officer T. L. (Lev) Reddick, shot to death in 1928 while questioning the driver of an auto thought to have been a stolen vehicle.

Another police-related tragedy came across more as an embarrassment than anything else. The date this time was March 1924. L. C. (Leafter) Jenkins, about 35, who hailed from Charlotte and had been Thomasville police chief only four months, was jailed for the murder of a woman on East Guilford Street. The chief identified her as his wife, when in fact she was his girlfriend who had been threatening to return to her husband. Jenkins said she shot herself but the court found Jenkins to be the shooter and sent him off to prison for 25-30 years.

By 1920 a full recovery from both World War I and the devastating Spanish infuenza epidemic of 1918 was well under way in Thomasville and the rest of the country. The flu had taken as many American lives as trench warfare in France, and one had evoked about as much sympathy for its victims as the other. This was apparent in a newspaper account of a raid aimed at destroying a still operating in

20

The Mock Hotel with more than 40 rooms is shown on this 1927 C. R. Thomas post card, a Thomasville landmark owned and operated by Mrs. John A. (Minnie) Mock (later Mrs. W. H. McIntyre). Erected around 1892 by Mrs. Mock, it was a Thomasville social center for quite a long time. Clubs held luncheon and dinner meetings there. In 1939, about 10 years after the death of Mrs. McIntyre, the hotel burned down. One of the guests lost his life in the fire.

Conrad Hill Township, some 10 miles southwest of Thomasville. The account said "It was a 165-gallon capacity, of copper, and well constructed. A note pinned to the still requested that it not be bothered, as every drop of the liquor being manufactured is being used by the influenza sufferers in High Point and Thomasville, that no one profited by the running of the stilll as the liquor was given absolutely free to the sick people ..."

As recorded by noted essayist-commentator Gerald Johnson, who grew up in Thomasville, the 1920s in The Chair Town were "vibrantly, tingly alive." A night-time fire wiped out the town's first and only public school on Good Friday 1922, Thomasville Graded, that is, built in 1902. While a new one was taking shape, the Opera House on the second floor over the drug store on the northwest corner of the Town Square served school children as a makeshift gymnasium. Activities therein included boys and girls basketball. Two of the girls's first-stringers were sisters, and members of a Thomasville family of moment, Evelyn and Clarice Peacock.

A new school, modern in every detail, would open within a year. Until then, children attended classes at churches and other places. It was said the fire did not deny students a single day of instruction.

The new one rose up from the ashes of the old. Although never proved, townspeople accepted that someone had set the fire, and, instead of committing the crime of arson, did the public a favor. The spectacular blaze settled a fiery debate over whether to place a new school on the site of the existing one, an option in the planning being done to update facilities and alleviate overcrowding, or relocate its replacement on a lot on Colonial Drive. The fire insurance pay-off ($47,000) covered a sizeable part of the cost of new construction. Bricks from the old school were cleaned up and used to erect the town's first fire station, on

22

MOCK HOTEL AND SOUTHERN RAILWAY STATION, THOMASVILLE, N. C.

This 1929 C. R. Thomas post card ties together two of Thomasville's centers of activity during the Twenties, the Southern Railway passenger station and the Mock Hotel. For visitors arriving by train during that time, hotel accommodations were no more than a step or two away. The station was a West Main Street fixture until 1975 but the hotel burned down in 1939.

East Guilford at Commerce Street. And the City Council quit stalling. It rushed up the acquisition of the town's first store-bought fire truck, a 1922-model LaFrance that, while no longer in service, of course, is fully restored and kept on display by today's Thomasville Fire Department.

Prof. Hauss had arrived just as that first school began its second year, and then lorded it over the education of the town's youth until his departure -- a temporary absence, it turned out -- 25 years later. A mere whisp of a man, he managed to hold the attention of students by interacting his iron will with a barrel of hickory switches. George L. Hundley, a member of the school's Class of 1925 who went on to be successful in banking, to serve as Thomasville mayor, state senator and highway commissioner, recollected that sometimes there were as many as two dozen stout discipline enhancers in the barrel, kept in a room near Hauss's office. The superintendent had a firm grip on one of the stoutest of these one day when confronting George and a classmate after they had been caught using profanity on the school playground. Hauss asked the classmate to speak the word that had landed him in trouble. The teacher who arrested the two lads had said it was so disgusting she couldn't repeat it. The classmate hestitated. Hauss tried coaxing, and finally got his answer, except the boy spelled it out. He was rewarded for being delicate. On his bare legs he was stung only two or three times by Hauss's switch. George proved to be more forthright. When it came his turn, he readily blurted out his indiscretion. Hauss was shocked, and somewhat irritated. He felt the example of waywardness standing before him was being purposely shocking. So poor George received the maximum. Or his naked bottom did. Ten authoritarian whacks. A bit later, George confessed to a friend, "Today, Prof. Hauss taught me to spell."

24

Southern Railway Passenger Station, Thomasville, N. C.

The Southern Railway passenger depot, pictured on this post card, was built in 1911-12. After failure of an effort to make it a museum, and long after the decline in passenger use of the rails, the building was demolished, in the year 1975. Passenger service over the Southern tracks is still alive but quite limited. Boarding a train, or debarking, is no longer possible in Thomasville.

Thanks to a Thomasville attorney, Howell Kyser, school children got to meet a rising star in the entertainment world. Howell, or Hal, had a brother, Kay Kyser, who first made a name for himself as a cheerleader at the University of North Carolina, then, although he could neither read music nor play an instrument, formed a dance band in Chapel Hill. He was highly visible there, in his Model-T roadster named "Passion" (it was so quick to heat up). Sometimes when in Thomasville to see his brother, Kay would put in an appearance at the local school, mainly to visit briefly with Hal's children. On at least one occasion he brought along his musicians. A newspaper reported "Kay Kyser with his orchestra of Chapel Hill, made a hit in the school auditorium Friday evening (December 1, 1927) ... The entertainment was spoken of as the best and most enjoyable that has stopped here in months."

As in many places, the first radio broadcasts to reach Thomasville arrived in a cigar box, or by way of a crystal set, complete with earphones. This marvelous gadget, assembled by resourceful Earl Fritts, usually could pick up KDKA in Pittsburgh once this station hit the airways in 1920 with regular programming. In recognition of his pioneering effort, the owner of the Thomasville cigar box was dubbed "Radio" Fritts, and he was known as that as long as he lived.

Radio began sweeping the country. Becoming a fixture in a great many Thomasville living rooms was the console-style Atwater-Kent radio that magnificently let in the outside world. Joining in to influence manners and morals were the films being shown at a new type of downtown attraction, Lee Amusement Co., along with a few publications, not the least of which were *The Saturday Evening Post* and the Sears & Roebuck catalog. Frances Millis Bevan remembers, as a high schooler, being entranced by lover-boy Rudolph Valentino, and suitably embarrassed

1724 Freight Depot, Thomasville, N.C

In the post card picture here, dozens of newly made chairs are stacked at the Southern Railway freight depot in Thomasville to await shipment. The depot served many years, until its demolition in 1975, the same day as the passenger depot's. The freight depot office portion, Thomasville's first passenger station, was saved and restored. Located on West Main Street and now a community center, it is North Carolina's oldest railroad passenger station.

as well, while attending a showing of the mildly risque silent film "The Sheik" at the Opera House during the time it briefly doubled as the local cinema.

When it came time to put up a building exclusively for the showing of moving pictures, Thomasville did it in a big way. Local entrepreneur Charles F. Finch, a leading furniture manufacturer, had it erected on, where else? Salem Street, a somewhat palatial structure with a baroque look. Finch therefore had it named The Palace. One of those generating oratory on opening night in February 1924, Thomasville banker Roby L. Pope, preferred to characterize the Salem Street spectacle as a temple, "a temple of pleasure," in fact. A full house applauded its approval, then it settled back to watch -- a silent film -- "Her Temporary Husband." The Palace was the main movie house until the day it closed, in January 1959, in a period when movie-going in Thomasville had gone into remission.

Pleasure was being experienced at a faster beat, and, to keep up, the dancers -- the flappers included -- created "The Varsity Drag," "The Shimmey," "The Turkey Trot" and "The Buzzard Lope," but these crazes, all of them sensuous and suggestive styles of tripping across the dance floor, were on the wane by the time radio fans from coast-to-coast began forming their attachment to Kay Kyser and his catchy tunes.

Presence of the auto was spreading, emancipating great numbers of people. Even so, Thomasville did not easily accept that the auto had the horse on the run, that the age of horseless transportation had come. As late as 1915 the Town Council appropriated funds to install a fountain and watering trough on Salem Street. Still being enforced was a town ordinance discouraging behavior that might spook the old gray mare. It decreed that "Any person who shall roll or cause to be rolled any kind of hogshead or barrel upon the streets or sidewalks of the town in view of

In 1926, The U. S. Post Office in Thomasville, upon vacating a location on Salem Street, occupied the newly completed structure shown on this 1927 C. R. Thomas post card. It was Thomasville's first federal building. A new federal building-post office, the one still in use, was opened in 1963. Since 1972, the building pictured has been city-owned. Presently, it houses the city department of recreation.

any horse or mule in the streets shall be fined $1." (The town code of that period reined in other what now seem to be quaint activities. One of its sections advised "It shall be unlawful for any person, firm or corporation either to exhibit, or cause or permit to be exhibited, any hypnotized person or persons in the show window of any business house on any street of the Town of Thomasville, or in any other place where such hypnotized person can be seen from the streets or sidewalks.")

Local government displayed little inclination to conclude its own dependency on horses and mules. As late as 1953 a team of mules, "George" and "Tom", when hitched to a flat-bottomed wagon, was being used in the cleaning of debris from street gutters. A new city manager, Everett W. Schadt, was astonished. He promptly declared the team surplus property. At a public auction, Grady Hooker of Thomasville became owner of the animals and their wagon with a high bid of $152.50, whereupon Schadt declared that at long last Thomasville had progressed beyond the horse-and-buggy era.

Thomasville had become electrified by Southern Public Utilities (later Duke Power) as of about 1910. Just a year later, once a $75,000 bond issue had been authorized, a waterworks and sewer system were built, then some Thomasville families had running water and indoor plumbing to go along with electric lights. Paving of downtown streets and sidewalks was just one more way in which Thomasville became citified by the start of World War I and prepared for the Twenties to roar in.

As it grew larger, it grew messier. To slow this down, some of the women formed the Civic Improvement League, in 1909, and set out to make the town more sanitary as well as prettier. While they were not able to abolish the Hog Lot, an ugly catch-all, multi-purpose clearing on a corner of the Town Square, within two years

In 1901, a year after its organization, Cramer Furniture Co. was claiming to be the second largest furniture manufacturer in the South, and by 1913, when it was comprised of several plants, the South's largest and most thriving enterprise. John T. Cramer was its president. On this C. R. Thomas post card is probably the company's principal plant. Everything was sold to Thomasville Chair Co. in 1914.

the league had persuaded the Town Council to pass an ordinance requiring downtown merchants to sweep and otherwise clean the sidewalks in front of their businesses each and every Saturday night.

Both socializing and nurturing of the intellect were accomplished with the formation of the Phi Beta Club in 1916. Its outreach had severe limitations, however. Membership in this pioneer book study group was restricted to a mere dozen of Thomasville's most fashionable ladies. They assembled at regular intervals to exchange and evaluate reading matter and to ponder the news of the day. Its foundation was rock-like. The club remains hale and hearty today, still traditionally exclusive, the oldest social organization in the city.

More culture began to seep in with the formation in 1919 of the first so-called civic club, the Thomasville Woman's Club (also still very much alive). It was comprised of three departments, social service, civic, and music. Club projects included beautifying City Cemetery, establishing a curfew to protect the community's young people, and cleaner and neater outhouses. Much of the city was still out of reach of city sewerage. During a campaign in October 1920 to upgrade the "little brown shack out back," Thomasville experimented with the double-concrete vault model as a replacement for the old-style open pit, hoping to reduce Thomasville's violations of state sanitary laws. The mayor, J. C. Green, a city councilman, Dr. J. W. Peacock, and other city officials inspected a concrete vault installation on the property of Fred Black of Lexington Road and then, according to the local newspaper, declared the vault "solves the question for Thomasville." A later report indicated this progressive design was being widely adopted in The Chair Town.

This C. R. Thomas post card issued in 1929 bears a photo of the Thomasville Chair Co. unit given the designation Plant C (C for Cramer Furniture, the plant's originator). A section of the unit served as the Thomasville Chair office building. Since 1961, Thomasville Chair, formed in 1904, has been Thomasville Furniture Industries, one of the world's largest producers of fine household furnishings.

Apparently it was the intent to beautify City Cemetery that gave rise to the Cemetery Association of Thomasville, which assumed management of these burial grounds from local government, probably in the expectation that appearance and operation would greatly improve. The cemetery was right where John W. Thomas said it should be when he laid out the town around 1852 and provided space for it on East Guilford Street. But after two or three years the association was ready for and welcomed a return to local government control. In November 1924 City Hall reassumed responsibility and has been in charge ever since. The city sold the last of the grave plots some 50 years ago.

The return to City Hall control came a year after R M. (Bob) Cooksey, a civil engineer from Baltimore, was hired as city manager. These people move about a lot but Cooksey was manager in Thomasville for 29 years. When he retired in 1952 only one or two others in the United States had been a city manager at the same station for any longer.

Townspeople were pleased when the Masons got around to making their lodge building on Randolph Street more presentable, the one that was erected in 1873 and served for quite a few years also as the town's first public school. After a thorough remodeling in 1923 it became an attractive, architecturally pleasing structure of brick, the pride of Thomasville Lodge No. 214, Ancient Free and Accepted Masons, one of the oldest organizations in town (chartered in December 1860), a fraternal order that attracted a number of the rich and the powerful in Thomasville.

Tobacco crops were putting more cash in the pockets of area farmers. Nearby in Johnsontown, John F. Sechriest, in 1925, harvested one-and-a-quarter acres of leaf and sold it at a Winston-Salem market for a cool one thousand dollars.

The Page Trust Co. bank pictured on this C. R. Thomas post card issued in 1927 occupied a building on the east side of the first block of Salem Street that formerly had housed banking operations. A branch of Page Trust Co. of Aberdeen, it opened in November 1923, then after closing in March 1933 in observance of the national Bank Holiday it did not reopen.

An annual street festival had been invented in 1908, when such galas were quite rare, mainly to lure Mr. Sechriest and others downtown from outlying areas to spend more of their hard-earned money with local merchants. It was called Everybody's Day and hours of entertainment were provided in the Fall in many forms, such as balloon ascensions and auto races over downtown streets (the racing madness was abolished after a driver attempting a U-turn on East Main Street lost control of his vehicle and he was fatally injured). The festival was staged each year until 1924, then was revived in 1946 and has been held most years ever since. In 1920 a festival feature was a match in which Greensboro High School defeated Salisbury High 20-6 in what went down in the record books as the first regulation football game ever to be played in Thomasville. Also in 1920, a successor to the Civic Improvement League, or the Work & Win Club, sponsored a better baby show held under the supervision of Thomasville's Dr. R. V. Yokeley, also county health officer. Prizes were offered. In one phase of competition, a prize of $5 went to "The blackest Negro baby in Davidson County."
        People of color made up 15 to 20 per cent of the local population, which was fairly typical of many small North Carolina communities. They were not in the habit of crossing a quite distinct color line. Black men dug the ditches, cleaned out the barns, and then when a hospital was established they administered the enemas. The black women scrubbed the floors and did the ironing. Some were employed as a nanny, so they raised white children as well as their own. Whites at nearby Brokaw Castle thought a game they played at festive affairs helped the needy. They gave silver dollars to small black children. But to strike it rich the tots had to jump into great open hogsheads of white flour into which the coins had been tossed, then had to search for them.

In this C. R. Thomas post card issued in 1927, the lobby of First National Bank, founded in 1907, is lined on each side by stations for tellers who functioned in the safety of "cages." The lobby was the focal point of the three-story bank building erected on Salem Street in 1922, on the site of First National's first home. The City of Thomasville gained title to the building in 1991 and today it is the City Hall.

Rotary, the second civic club, was organized in 1922. Robert Rapp, an Amazon mill official, was the first new member after Rotary was chartered. Club meetings, held at the Mock Hotel, had not yet grown stuffy. At the conclusion of his induction, Rapp was required by his sponsor, Frank S. Lambeth, to place his right forefinger on top of his head, and spin about while singing "I'm a little prairie flower, growing wilder by the hour." Then President T. Austin Finch presented him with the Rotary ring, a tap of his gavel on the Rotary gong.

There was not a proper library until a branch of the county system was opened in 1928.

That was long after C. R. Thomas, the drug store man, undertook to make a little money by way of picture-taking, usually an activity of the young people. They snapped one another for the fun of it. In 1907, Thomas began producing post cards featuring photographs of Thomasville structures and objects. These would become a valuable pictorial record of that period. A paragraph in the Thomasville news column of the issue of *The Dispatch* of Lexington dated March 13, 1907, read: "C. R. Thomas, the druggist, has just received about one dozen different views of Thomasville on postal cards and now has souvenir cards of the town for sale -- 2 for 5 cents." In fact, Thomas was advertising himself. He was the writer of the column of news in *The Dispatch* about Thomasville. What's more, *The Dispatch*'s Thomasville bureau and Thomas's drug store were one and the same.

38

STREET SCENE, EVERYBODY'S DAY.
THOMASVILLE, N.C.

The producer of this post card was J. M. Morris & Son Co., a Thomasville general store. It shows an Everybody's Day parade as it moved along a Thomasville dirt street. Those outfront appear to be members of a military organization. Everybody's Day originated in 1908 and has been held most years since then. A parade remains one of its features.

Part Two

The Thomasville downtown area, the stem of which always has been Salem Street, was hemmed in by residences, of course. The most elegant homes faced the railroad that evenly split the town, while most of the factories were concentrated south of the tracks -- although not out of reach of a spurline. Outlying neighborhoods were developing, such as Rabbit Quarter to the west, Onion Hill to the south, and Monkey Hollow to the east. The latter was only two or three blocks from Slimey Corner, a sharp bend in National Highway (formerly Highway No. 10) that ressembled a quagmire in exeedingly wet weather.

That of Dr. C. A. Julian's was perhaps the most regal of the residences that looked out on the railroad. This one became fixed in the memory of that man of letters, Gerald Johnson. Once when dwelling on growing up in Thomasville in the early 1900s, he wrote: "I have ... seen the columns of the Madeleine in Paris, and the circle of the monoliths in the National Gallery of Art in Washington, but they impressed no less than the columns on Dr. Julian's house, fifty years ago."

To R. L. Lambeth goes the honor of being first to own an Eastman Kodak camera. No doubt Dr. Julian's place consumed some of his film.

Thomasville was a church-going community. Church members were mainly Methodists and Baptists. A tent revival was something the "shouting Methodists" eagerly

A notation on this post card of the Thomasville Female College suggests the woman in the buggy is Mary Gray, thought to have been an instructor at the college. The building, erected in 1857, was at first the Glen Anna Female Seminary. It flourished as a girls finishing school until the late 1880s. Since 1913 this East Main Street structure has housed manufacturing operations. It was known much of that time as Ragan Knitting Mills.

awaited whenever the visiting tent preacher was to be the Rev. Jim Green, a Methodist himself. One that he conducted soon after the sensational shooting in which Dr. Peacock took the life of Police Chief J. E. Taylor, the mother of Thomasville calamities, went on and on, for five weeks. A newspaper account ranked it as "the greatest religious revival in the history of the town ... it came when it was needed the most." In round figures, overall attendance was 40,000, "professions" 600, and the gain in local church membership 200. Most important, revival attendees made the collection jars jingle merrily with $8,249.22. This included the $900 contributed by members of Main Street Methodist Church expressly to pay for a gift to the church pastor, the Rev. R. G. Tuttle. The gift, presented the day after the revival ended, was a new Ford sedan purchased from the local Ford dealer, G. W. Lyles. It came fully equipped -- bumper, number (meaning license plate), almost everything. Without charge Mr. Lyles added a spare tire. A little money was left over, a sum promptly spent at the Main Street Methodist parsonage to pay for constructing a garage to house the gift.

Life in the Chair Town was somewhat flavored and swayed by both the Thomasville Baptist Orphanage and an institution of a far different nature, the Thomasville Shooting Club. At times more than 500 youngsters were under the eagle-eyed care of the first "church" shelter for orphans in North Carolina, a little town of its own of several hundred acres (including "Paradise Hill," once a Negro camp-meeting site). The staff helped stock Thomasville positions of leadership, and Thomasville government was thankful it could draw on the orphanage's munificent deep well to undergird the town's fledgling water system.

Until renamed Mills Home after an expansion into other locales and venturing forth to become one of the nation's most respected child-care programs (Baptist

42

The building that housed the Thomasville Baptist Orphanage library, pictured on this 1927 C. R. Thomas post card, added beauty to the institution's grounds. It was built in 1908, then demolished in 1965 -- the year, on the same spot, the present-day orphanage library was constructed. The old one was equipped with a fire-proof vault for the safe-keeping of TBO records. Library doors were closed to "any novel that is not of a pure and elevating character."

Children's Homes of North Carolina), it was simply "The Orphanage," noted among other things for its discipline and gifted athletes. There were many forms and degrees of measures to encourage the young to be obedient and stay out of trouble. Punishment for a lad creating a worrisome distraction at mealtime might have been a trip to the cow barn with a fly swatter. When allowed to return would have depended on how soon he could prove he killed 500 flies. A 1922 graduate of the orphanage high school, Johnny Allen, worked his way up to the big leagues. He then pitched for several clubs, including the Cleveland Indians, Brooklyn Dodgers and New York Giants, and starred on the mound for the Yankees when they won the 1932 World Series.

After the Palace Theater opened in 1924, a common sight was dozens of orphans walking single-file to the center of town, and later once they had been admitted free to the theater for a special showing of a movie, marching back to the orphanage grounds.

During his Christmas Day sermon in 1925 the pastor of the orphanage's church, the Rev. E. Norfleet Gardner, paused to pay his respects to members, the young and the old, so dependent on the generosity of others, for the support they themselves had shown a range of causes during the year ending. "Frequently have come to us," he said, "special calls: The memorial window at Rich Fork (Baptist Church) to J. H. Mills (orphanage founder), aid for the church building of our colored brethren and sisters in Thomasville, the relief of the stricken coal miners in Cove Glen, North Carolina, the Anti-Saloon League, famine in the Near East, the recent Christmas love offering of considerably more than $200 to lift the burden of debt from our foreign missions work, and other objects to which you have contributed so gladly that there has not been heard an

44

The ox-and-cart conveyance being ridden by Thomasville Baptist Orphanage children in this post card that predates 1910 was used to transport luggage and freight between the orphanage and the Thomasville railroad depot. "Old Buck" pulled the cart a number of years, or until a change to other forms of transportation about 1909. Rather than being put out to pasture, he was fattened up, slaughtered, and the children were favored with a meal of beef, a rare treat back then.

expression of regret from anyone for the least sum given to any of these needs."

The shooting club made it possible for Thomasville to change its focus from the needy to the filthy rich. World-renown explorers, auto makers, those turning huge profits in oil, railroad builders from the Northwest were club members and guests of members -- the Goulds, Rockefellers, Biddles and Colgates. The clubhouse, where they lodged when not out banging away excitedly at quail flushed from Davidson County fields, was the 20-room mansion on West Main Street, across from the depot, that had been acquired in 1894 from the man who built it, Ped Thomas. Some members arrived in Pullman cars, which they parked at the depot for the duration. From neighboring farmers the club leased the hunting rights on 60,000 acres. Some of Thomasville's most prominent citizens were hunting-dog trainers. Wesley Veach was one of those who picked up pocket change by helping to rid the skies of some of the quail's predators. He was paid a bonus by club Manager Archie Primm when he showed up with an eagle he had gunned down. Usually Primm's bounties were for smaller raptors. One season he "bought" 250 hawks.

The manager had Veach's eagle mounted and then put on display at the clubhouse.

Frank H. Fleer, the chewing gum king from Philadelphia, came to Thomasville to hunt quail, then decided to stay on much of each year. He purchased what was once the country estate at Fair Grove of Thomasville founder John W. Thomas, created a model farm there and named it Cedar Lodge. Of German descent, Fleer looked out one day to find a group of protesters in his front yard. World War I was at its zenith. A flag was flying from a pole attached to the front of the house. Fleer had difficulty

The dining hall at Thomasville Baptist Orphanage was a sturdy, attractive building. Pictured on this post card, it was constructed in 1904 and used until the serving of meals at a central location was discontinued. Barely visible near the front steps is the bell, at top of a pole, that was rung to signal a meal was ready to be put on the tables. The building no longer stands.

convincing the complainers that he was proudly displaying his family coat of arms, not the ensignia of Kaiser Bill.

A local newspaper once identified Fleer as "the wealthiest citizen in Davidson County." It reported in May 1917 that he had offered the federal government 2,000 acres of his estate, a tract within two miles of Thomasville, as a location for a German prisoner-of-war camp. There was no reported protest this time. The newspaper observed "It will be very agreeable to our people if the government sees fit to settle the Teutons near us. We will be glad to profit by their efficiency." But what the government saw fit to do was to decline Fleer's offer.

He was fond of riding horseback with Alice, one of his daughters. On one of their outings they explored a portion of Three-Hat Mountain, a set of modest promontories some 12 miles southwest of Thomasville. The daughter was taken with the beauty of the surroundings and wished some of it were her very own. A few days later her father presented her with a deed for one of the mountain's three "hats."

Thomasville Telephone erected an attractive two-story sandstone building in 1917, on Salem Street, naturally. The company had introduced the radical automatic dial system in 1911, making Thomasville one of the first cities in North Carolina to have access to this magic. It did not become North State Telephone, by way of a merger, until 1935. The 1920 Thomasville Telephone directory explained, under Instructions to Subscribers, "We are willing to furnish the TIME only to those who wish to set their timepieces. Please do not ask the time of day for any other purpose." Inside, the telephone number for the orphanage was 1, for Dr. Peacock's office 72.

Nearly as useful as the telephone was Western Union Telegraph. Mrs. Vera Green Phillips was the manager of the local office for almost a half century. The

First Baptist Church, Thomasville, North Carolina

First Baptist has been one of Thomasville's strongest churches throughout the life of the community. It erected the building shown on this post card on Randolph Street in 1913. Fifty years later, in 1963, the congregation removed it, and in its place constructed a larger, finer building, the one in use today.

young man who delivered her telegrams on a bicycle, Paul Shore, grew up to be a longtime Thomasville police chief. Sometimes, if the message was a heart-breaker, Vera delivered it herself, along with her tender condolences.

The County Seat once in a while would relax its firm control over the politics of the realm and indulge the election of a Thomasville resident to state office. Attorney B. W. Parham, son-in-law of orphanage editor Archibald Johnson, who was the father of Gerald, went to the state house in 1911. So did A. Mack Hiatt, in 1919, and A. Homer Ragan, manufacturer and developer, in 1929. Election to the state senate in 1921 put J. Walter Lambeth on the road to a seat in Congress. Son of John Lambeth and nephew of Frank Lambeth, he served four terms in the U. S. House, 1931-39, the only person from Thomasville ever to hold elective office on Capitol Hill. The outbreak of World War II scuttled the plan of President Franklin D. Roosevelt to make him the U. S. ambassador to Austria.

The pioneer in furniture-making, D. S. Westmoreland, had a brother, J. F. Westmoreland, who pioneered newspaper-publishing. He was owner and editor of the first Thomasville paper appearing regularly and continuously. To begin with, in 1890, it was *The News*, a weekly, but then for a long time it went by *The Times*. While in Raleigh in 1895, serving a term in the state Senate, Westmoreland suffered a stroke. After that and until his death in 1913 he edited his paper from a wheelchair. A heavy-set individual, in little black skull cap and goatee, he was the most recognizable fixture on Randolph Street's Westmoreland Hill, the location of the newspaper office.

Other Westmorelands kept *The Times* limping along until 1926, despite competition from *The Davidsonian*, which was published from 1910 to 1913, then *The Chairtown News*, which debuted in 1920 under the ownership of furniture manufacturer Charles F. Finch. Once

Main Street Methodist Church's building was about 20 years old when photographed for this C. R. Thomas post card issued in 1927. Main Street merged with Community Methodist Church in 1947 to form Memorial, and in 1951 the doors of the beautiful Memorial Methodist Church building on Randolph Street first opened. Neither the Main Street nor Community building is still standing.

when Finch was in Chicago on furniture business, someone ridiculed the newspaper he was reading, a copy of *The Times*. Supposedly it was then that he decided to go back home and establish a paper people would praise. In 1926 he purchased *The Times* and combined it with his paper to form *The News-Times*. Soon thereafter, he quit the publishing business. Under other owners and as a semi-weekly *The News-Times* was Thomasville's principal paper for the next 20 years. Other mergers followed, making it possible for today's tri-weekly *Thomasville Times* to claim it is directly descended from Thomasville's first newspaper.

The post office hopped about on Salem Street until 1913 when it settled down in the Finch Block (erected in 1904). The next move did not take place until it occupied the federal building on East Main Street at the time it was completed in 1926. Two years later, the delivery of mail to homes inside the city began. The first two carriers were Austin Elliott, who had been a school teacher, and C. J. Harris, a farmer. Both World War I veterans, they won their jobs by scoring highest on a test taken by 25 others. The first day, January 2, 1928, Elliott set out to serve all the addresses on the northside of the Southern's mainline and Harris those on the southside. This they did for the next 18 years, the only carriers, making morning and afternoon deliveries each weekday and mornings only on Saturday.

There was no city hall until 1938. Design of this first one, on West Guilford Street, made it possible to bring together all city offices, a fire station, police station, jail, courtroom, and public library -- and to provide the first public restrooms, in the basement, whites only. For most of the 1920s, however, the jail was a tiny brick building, somewhat a one-celler, set back from stores facing East Main and those facing Salem Street (to some it was the "Crutchfield Jail," apparently an allusion to its proximity to

52

A number of Thomasville's movers and shakers belonged to Main Street Methodist Church's Baraca Class, whose membership can be found on this post card. The class was organized in 1910 with 23 members. Soon there were 200. For many years the class was a force for good in the community. It was the forerunner of today's R. L. Pope Bible Class at Memorial United Methodist Church.

Crutchfield Hardware Store). Anything of greater dimensions might have been a waste. A 1922 newspaper article described Thomasville as a town with "almost no need for a jail." Anyway, the county government lockup in Lexington was available to detain bigtime trouble-makers.

Until 1938, the fire station remained on East Guilford, the one built of brick from the schoolhouse fire. It served as a comfortable home for the 1922 store-bought fire truck and a place for volunteer firemen to congregate and tell tall tales. They relived the period in which they pulled cumbersome handreels of hose to the scene of fires and then the uncertainties imposed by the successor to the reels, the Ford that had been transformed into a small, lightweight hose conveyance -- actually the town's first fire truck. In responding to an alarm one night, they threw open the doors to the garage housing the Ford only to discover it had four flat tires. Yet, the volunteers were only momentarily deflated. They speedily and rather ingeniously rigged up something not unlike a stretcher, or litter, and bodily carried the truck, hose and all, to where a fire was raging.

During this time, city offices and the courtroom could be found by climbing the steep flight of steps beside Thomasville Drug Store to the second floor of the Finch Block, or Finch Building. The offices and courtroom opened off a hallway. Another office there, of course, over the drug store, was the one from which Dr. J. W. Peacock launched the lethal loads of buckshot that found and felled an unsuspecting Police Chief J. E. Taylor.

Factory whistles kept Thomasville on its toes. They did more than signal it was time to go to work, how long to pause for lunch, and when to go home. Long, steady blasts meant either something had gone wrong, such as a breakdown in plant machinery that posed a threat to the workforce, or something good, such as the end of a war. Best known of these was "The Wildcat" at Standard Chair,

54

A view of Thomasville Graded School is provided by this post card, postmarked Thomasville 1913 on its address side. The building, constructed in 1902 with revenue from a $10,000 Town of Thomasville bond issue, occupied a tract bounded by East Main Street, Taylor Street, Montlieu Avenue and School Street. After it burned down in 1922, it was replaced within a year by a bigger, better Main Street School.

so named because when wide open it howled like a wounded bobcat. A Standard nightwatchman set it to screeching one evening when he thought he had seen that a nearby factory had caught fire. It happened in a period when a rash of small fires suggested a firebug was busy. But the watchman had alarmed a large part of the community for nothing. After sounding off for maybe five minutes, the whistle was gagged and the red-faced watchman hung down his head. Instead of flames, he had seen a full moon beginning to rise.

Whistles were joined by two sirens in the early 1920s, one an accessory on the city's first factory-made fire engine and the other on the city's first ambulance. The latter was a purchase of J. C. Green's funeral home. For another few years, Green continued to rely on a team of handsome black horses to wheel his hearse from place to place.

The nearest hospital was still in High Point. But in 1926 Dr. R. V. Yokeley and Dr. R. G. Jennings opened a clinic on the third floor of the First National Bank Building. Dr. C. H. Phillips had an office in the same building. His equipment included a crude X-ray machine, possibly the one that had been owned by Dr. Peacock, who could claim to have had in his possession Thomasville's first X-ray. One of Dr. Phillips's patients voiced a fear the physician announced his charges for an X-ray only after having X-rayed his patients's wallets.

A newspaper reported the clinic could set up as many as 15 beds for the sick if "the necessity arises. The rooms are all beautifully arranged, including the operating room, steam heat, the sanitation perfect, sunlight delightful. Hospital experts have looked into this situation and pronounce it o. k. for a small hospital." Dr. J. T. Burrus of High Point was on call to do difficult surgery.

Taking the place of Thomasville Graded School after it was destroyed by fire in 1922 was the structure on this C. R. Thomas post card issued in 1927. Identification on the card is incorrect. It was always known as Main Street School, named for its location, East Main Street, until lower grades were moved to other locations and it became both Main Street High School and Thomasville High.

Somehow Dr. Jennings succeeded in making it fashionable, or at least advisable, among the young people to undergo tonsillectomies at the clinic. To have one's tonsils removed was to be part of the "in" crowd. The price for being stylish was not considerable to be unreasonable. Only $25 went into Dr. Jennings's pocket each time one's tonsils came out.

Construction on Thomasville's first real hospital, one with 30 beds, began in 1929. Community-owned and non-profit, City Memorial opened the next year, at a cost of $105,000. Brothers George and Doak Finch, young furniture manufacturers, contributed $40,000 of that total. This gift was the sum netted from a law suit against the Southern Railway as result of the death of another Finch brother, Brown, also a young furniture executive. He died instantly in March 1925 when a crack Southern passenger train crashed into his car at a Thomasville crossing. The railroad, which argued that Brown was negligent, was sued by George and Doak, Brown's executors, for $252,000, thought to be at the time the most ever sought in this country in a wrongful death action. Even the $40,000 settlement was viewed as exorbitant. Brown's father, T. J. Finch, died of natural causes in July 1929, several months before the suit was resolved.

Brown's death set off the loudest, most anguished outcry yet for either an underpass or overpass so traffic could be guaranteed safe passage when it was moving from one side of the railroad's mainline to the other. Accidents at the grade crossings were increasing frightfully as the number of train trips through town grew and Thomasville's population gained. The pleas for protection heard each time the trains killed somebody were not answered, however, until 1970, when the city's first and only underpass for vehicles was opened. Since then a railroad crossing death has been most unusual.

Behind a screen of trees on this C. R. Thomas post card issued in 1929 is Colonial Drive Elementary School. For years it was the custom of education leaders to put the location of the school in the school's name. Colonial Drive, now a center of county government services, was built in 1928 as Thomasville's second public school building. It eased the overcrowding at Main Street.

Most of the coming and going was in and out of the Southern Railway passenger depot. At the time of Brown's death 14 passenger trains -- plus no few freights -- made their way past the station every 24 hours. Some stopped, some didn't. Sleepers were among the cars of most, some of which, even back then, chugged all the way from New York City to New Orleans.

For Thomasville's other railroad, the town was indebted to a man of vision, one Capt. Milton Jones, who in 1905, with some of his wealth from the mining of precious metals in Montgomery County, had begun laying rails southward from Thomasville, partly to open sections of Southern Davidson to logging. In 1906, the Thomasville and Glen Anna (his homeplace bore the name Glen Anna Plantation) had been completed to Denton. By then Jones had purchased a two-cylinder Reo, the first auto in Thomasville with a gasoline engine. But the owner used it to tool along the tracks between Thomasville and Denton, not the dusty byways of The Chair Town. He had removed the Reo's wheels, then had replaced them with a set that had flanges. That is, railroad wheels. People in substantial numbers began to ride the same tracks when passenger service was inaugurated in late 1906.

After Jones's death in 1910, the line changed hands more than once, and branched out, to provide connections with High Point and High Rock. In 1924 it was given the name under which it operates today, the High Point, Thomasville & Denton Railroad, or HPT&DRR, which irreverant wags say stands if not for "Hog Path Through Davidson" then "Higgeley, Piggeley, Tiggeley Dee Railroad." Passenger service played out long ago, but before it did, HPT&DRR also translated as "High-Priced Ticket and a Damned Rough Ride."

"Consolidated" was part of the name of Fair Grove School in the beginning, as indicated in this C. R. Thomas card dated 1927. In opening in 1926 it was the consolidation of Fair Grove, Davidson Academy and Byerly Graded School. The Pilot consolidation in 1921 was Davidson County's first. Fair Grove and Pilot high schools became East Davidson in 1961. The building pictured here has been razed.

At the start of 1921, Thomasville was doing business with three banks, but by the end of that year, due to a mild recession, two had closed down, leaving only First National. The survivor had been making do with a small brick building on Salem Street. The next year, this structure was taken away and in its place there grew from the bank's surpluses a new First National building, the one in which the clinic was opened, an imposing three-story edifice that today remains as sturdy and attractive as ever, except that now it serves as the Thomasville City Hall.

The Bank of Thomasville, one of the two to fail in 1921, had occupied a building on the east side of the first block of Salem Street. Page Trust used the same space from 1923 until it also failed, in 1933. George L. Hundley chose this same location when organizing his State Industrial Bank in 1945. He was advised against it. After all, bad things happen in threes. But Hundley was not dissuaded, or intimidated. He vowed to make as much money in that place as the other two banks had lost. He did, and a lot more. He died a very rich man.

Others followed Capt. Milton Jones's lead and purchased autos. A census on June 12, 1912, credited Thomasville with 27 of these odd machines. Precisely one year later, the count was 70, as well as two auto repair garages. Therefore, the days of the livery stable were numbered. Three were thriving in 1903. Twenty years later, only Brack Wagner's had held on, and it hung around for only a brief period.

Blacksmith shops, on the other hand, lasted much longer.

Thomasville was slowly winning the war against ankle-deep mud. The first sidewalk was laid in 1905, along East Main from The Square to the Methodist church, or to Cemetery Street, and stepping stones were installed at several key street crossings. Motorists rejoiced when the

Construction of City Memorial Hospital, shown on this post card, started in 1929 and was concluded in 1930. A 31-bed non-profit facility owned by the community and governed by a self-perpetuating board of trustees, it was Thomasville's first true hospital. Community General opened in 1971, at which time City Memorial was closed and then sold. Located on Pine Street, it is now an apartment complex.

first street-paving came along soon thereafter. By 1925, Thomasville could boast of having 15 miles of concrete sidewalks and 13 miles of hard-surfaced thoroughfares.

There was a town band that gave concerts once in a while at the bandstand on the Town Commons. George Yow was the band's much applauded cornet player. If in Thomasville to make a speech, politicians oftentimes made the bandstand their platform. Once a year the R. C. Lee Riding Devices showed up. The merry-go-round and Ferris wheel would be erected at the corner of East Main and Cemetery streets and usually were in operation every night for a week. Mr. Lee always roomed at the Millis boarding house on Cemetery. One of the Millis girls, Frances, was riding the Ferris wheel one night with Ruth Primm. When it made one of its pauses, the girls could look down and about from the very top of the wheel. Ruth spotted the Bevan boys and pointed to them. It was the first time Frances ever saw Fred Bevan. Not long afterward they were married, and stayed married for more than 50 years.

Barring the economic downturn in 1921, times were pretty good through most of the Twenties. Prices continued to creep upward. In 1920 the Sanitary Barbershop found it necessary to increase the charge for a haircut from 25 to 35 cents. But most others held fast. A singe still went for 25 cents; massage 25 cents; peroxide steam 40 cents; and Glover's mange cure 50 cents.

Also downtown were a Sanitary Lunch and a Sanitary Pressing Club. By 1923 Central Motor Co. on East Main Street was selling Chevrolets, in competition with G. W. Lyles's Ford agency. Hinkle Milling on Randolph Street was contending that the best biscuits could be made with its Bride's Pride self-rising flour. A chiropractor in the Cates Building, Dr. Walter L. Fast, advertised "Health is Wealth." He was favorably located, a few doors from a bowling alley that J. C. Ellison operated for a short time. Among the

The founder of Thomasville, John W. Thomas, built the house shown on this post card in the first block of Thomasville's West Main street in 1857. It was later the home of a son, Dr. R. W. Thomas, and then a grandson, C. R. Thomas, drug store proprietor and producer of post cards. The imposing dwelling was torn down in the 1930s to make way for construction of a business building.

several grocery stores was Thomasville Store Co., also stocking shoes, notions, dry goods and ladies ready-to-wear. Grocers (and many front porches) were supplied by a total of five local dairies, Lambeth's, Everhart's, Southside, Sunnyside, and Jones's. Miss Eugenia Capitola Fife, remembered as Thomasville's first business woman, had a millinery shop downtown from 1900 to 1931 in which she created and customized lovely, fancy ladies hats, using ideas she picked up from French magazines and charging $10 and up per hat. J. C. Green, sometimes the town mayor, sold furniture and Victrolas and framed pictures on the first floor of his store on Salem Street and conducted his funeral home business on the second floor. Caskets made it up and back with the help of a small elevator, or lift, situated at the rear of the store building.

Some days the bell on the front door rang four or five times. The bored housewife didn't mind. It could have been the Jewel Tea salesman, the insurance agent working his debit, perhaps the pushy, premium-happy kid down the street hawking the most popular magazines -- *Collier's, Liberty, Saturday Evening Post.* Coming a knocking might have been an encyclopedia salesman or the Fuller Brush man with a choice of gifts -- vegetable brush, bottle brush or nail brush. Nothing deterred them, unless a measles quarantine sign had been attached to a porch post. Arriving at the back door was the 25-pound block of ice for the icebox -- soon to give way to the Kelvinator. Also, oftentimes the groceries ordered by phone. On Saturday morning, the friendly farmer making his usual delivery of fresh eggs and newly churned butter might visit for 10 minutes in the living room. Early on, goods in many shapes and forms reached the consumer in horse-drawn wagon. The children made friends with the horses, knew most by name.

The residence of business-civic leader J. W. Boyles, shown on this 1927 C. R. Thomas post card, has been demolished but for decades overlooked the Southern Railway from near the corner of West Main and Fisher Ferry streets. The site is occupied today by the U. S. Post Office building. The house was built for banker J. L. Armfield in 1907 by M. L. Ritchie, probably Thomasville's foremost building contractor at the time. It was still Boyles property when torn down in 1964.

Part Three

Away from the railroad tracks and the whine of furniture-making machinery, Thomasville neighborhoods were knee deep in peace and quiet. The small towns missed out on much of the roar of the Twenties. The dancing marathons, the noisy Ku Klux Klan rallies, and the throngs of spectators at flagpole-sittings were, for the most part, the doings of the heavily populated areas. If surrendering to extravagance, during the warm weather season, that is, a Chair Town couple might have headed out for Willowmoore Springs in the sticks 15 miles south for swimming, fishing or boating at the lake there, and, later on, dancing, square or round, at the pavilion. Willowmoore's Labor Day celebration in 1922 offered "boat races and all kinds of athletic contests" during the day and dancing to the music of the Tennessee Jazz Orchestra that night. Honeymooners could be accommodated at the hotel beside the lake. It was extensively patronized up until it burned down in 1943. Everybody had to sample the foul-tasting water from the several springs that allegedly imparted cures of all kinds.

But the typical Chair Town wage-earner never roamed far from home. He may never have run across a tourist court or a Burma-Shave sign.

The Mock was Thomasville's hotel in the 1920s, conveniently located across the street from the Southern Railway passenger station. Some guests stayed a month or

When this post card was issued in 1927 by C. R. Thomas the house shown was only five or six years old and the residence of the T. Austin Finches. Austin and wife, Ernestine Lambeth Finch, had it built soon after their marriage in 1919. The house, still widely admired, is located on East Main facing the Southern Railway. It has been a restaurant and put to other business uses since the death of the original owners.

more at a time. Organizations held dinner meetings there. It was the outgrowth of a residence enlarged to serve as a boarding house. Way back while the enlargement was taking place, the owner, John A. Mock, met tragedy when helping one of his guests board a train. He fell beneath one of the cars as the train began to move and it cost him his life. His wife, the former Minnie Wagoner, succeeded him, thereby also becoming a Thomasville business world upstart. The expansion was completed but the building burned down in 1892. Mrs. Mock replaced it with a three-story, 40-room structure. It remained a social center in Thomasville until, in 1939, it also burned down, not to be reborn. The last 10 years of its existence it was owned by Mr. and Mrs. Dewey and did business under the name of Baywood Hotel. The last fire claimed the life of a Baywood guest.

An example of a social event during the early 1920s was the annual Chrysanthemum Show at Main Street Methodist Church. It was managed by Mrs. Henry Rapp, wife of the former superintendent of a short-lived mining enterprise, the North Carolina Smelting Works. Show entries winning honors were auctioned off, with proceeds going to the church, after which an oyster supper was served.

At the center of what social whirl existed in Thomasville were the wealthy Lambeths and the well-to-do Finches. The Lambeths, related to Thomasville founder John W. Thomas, were chiefly among those organizing Standard Chair Co. in 1898, the first major furniture factory -- the one that raised the curtain on Thomasville's industrial age. It grew rapidly, in part by absorbing smaller chair plants that had popped up. In 1907 Frank S. Lambeth became sole owner. One son, Charles F. Lambeth, was president and another son, James E. Lambeth, was vice president. In 1921, Standard's five plants were making

The beautiful stone house on this 1927 C. R. Thomas post card was the residence of the Roby L. Pope family at the time the card was made. It was built around 1907 for Dr. J. W. Peacock and was the home of the Peacocks until not long before it was purchased by Mr. Pope in 1926. Still an outstanding structure among several attractive and historic houses on Thomasville's Salem Street, it is owned and occupied today by a Pope granddaughter, Mrs. Evelyn Waddell.

2,000 chairs a day but also an assortment of mission goods, box seats, diners, round-post diners, round-post rockers, maple porch rockers, swings and settees. There was not a broader line anywhere in the South.

Frank S. built a manion on Randolph Street that he gave the name of "Arlam," a coinage of his from Lambeth and from his wife's maiden name, Arnold. Even today (now the property of William Hinkle) it is one of Thomasville's grandest homes. And, as some would insist, still haunted by the ghost of a black man. Spinners of tales say he died at the house while the Frank Lambeths were the occupants, and that his death gave rise to questions that were never cleared up.

A pillar of Main Street Methodist Church, Frank could be counted on to manifest his pleasure when the congregation was called upon to stand up and render his favorite hymn, "Will There Be Any Stars in My Crown." He sang with gusto while rocking on his heels, clasped hands resting on his paunch.

Main Street Methodist was without question the holder of the title of foremost among Thomasville churches. It knew no peer until one of the monied Finches, Charles F., pulled out of First Methodist Protestant (located in Hogeye, which was a domain of the honest, the hard-working, the god-fearing -- some of them sawdust-encrusted furniture factory hands, some called "lint-heads," a dismal consequence of textiles mill employment) and in 1923 erected a church and community building near the Town Square, on Randolph Street, that was more awesome than any structure Thomasville had seen before. A memorial to Finch's wife, who died in 1921, it became the home of Community Methodist, which siphoned off a number of First church members, but was also a base for Boy Scouting and provided for establishing a public library. Plans were drawn for installing a gymnasium. Finch

RESIDENCE OF DR. CHAS. H. PHILLIPS, THOMASVILLE, N. C.

The impressive structure on yet another 1927 C. R. Thomas post card was built in the mid-1920s for Dr. Charles H. Phillips, who had moved his medical practice from Fuller's Mill to Thomasville a short time before. Later on it became the residence of an optometrist, Dr. Nat Walker, and his wife Pauline, a daughter of Dr. Phillips who worked tirelessly for Thomasville beautification. The house, in the Skiles Heights neighborhood, was demolished in 1998.

set forth the purpose of the building as a facility "to meet not only the demands of spiritual development but the natural demands of children for social and physical exercise."

He sold his half-interest in Thomasville Chair in 1925 to his brother, T. J. Finch, and T. J.'s sons (for $500,000, according to a newspaper report), after which he spent more time on the church project. Only about half of his dream came true, however. And what rivalry existed between Main Street and Community was extinguished by the merger of the two congregations, under the name of Memorial. Soon, a mere block from Community's last stand, a building rose up that was even more magnificent than Finch's monument. When it occupied this wonder in 1951, Memorial became the newest, most prominent, and never once since then has been in danger of losing that distinction.

What Finch had wrought recycled into the city-owned Civic Center. It experienced a high degree of use, especially the big auditorium, until 1976, the year a fire of unknown origin practically consumed it. Today, in its place stands the attractive Thomasville Public Library, enough of a community-plus to make a Charles F. Finch swell up with civic pride.

"It's the Lambeths who wear the brass buttons in Thomasville" had remained true only until Charles F. and his brother also had begun to succeed at buying up and consolidating small furniture plants. Before long these two were as influential as any others in the areas of manufacturing, commerce and local government. Townspeople made a sport of watching to see who would gain the higher ground. Soon after Charles F.'s interests had been acquired, T. J. and his sons -- T. Austin, Doak and George -- set about making the company an industry leader. When T. J. died in 1929, T. Austin became president and

The residence on this 1927 C. R. Thomas post card, that of A. Homer Ragan, no longer exists but was located in the 500 block of East Guilford Street. Ragan was a leader among those establishing Thomasville's manufacturing and financial firms in the early part of this century. He helped organize First National Bank, Peoples Building and Loan, and Ragan Knitting, and to lay the foundation for the Thomasville Fire Department.

before long had the company on the way to becoming what it is today, Thomasville Furniture Industries, one of the nation's most successful and best known sources of fine household furniture.

But as far back as 1919, the competition between the Lambeths and Finches had eased up. In that year, to the surprise but presumably the delight of virtually everybody, Ernestine, the beautiful daughter of John Lambeth (brother of Frank), became the bride of the handsome T. Austin. In a sense, the two tribes had merged. The newly-weds built a splendid house on East Main Street -- facing the railroad and on a tract once occupied by the Dr. Henry Rounsaville house -- that remains a Thomasville landmark to be admired until this day.

That an auspicious wedding was about to take place had been revealed at the end of the very first meeting of the Thomasville Woman's Club. In leaving, each member received a little card which told the date had been set for a Lambeth and Finch union.

Nothing equal to this had occurred since at the conclusion of the Civil War the love bug bit Jennie Thomas and caused her to succumb to matrimony. Jennie was the youngest daughter of Mary Lambeth Thomas and the founder of Thomasville, John W. Thomas. (When Mary was 17 and was being courted by John, 18, they eloped. They made their getaway on horseback.)

Jennie shocked everybody. She up and tied the knot with an officer in the despised Yankee army, John T. Cramer.

The officer was in the company of northern troops stationed briefly in Thomasville at the close of hostilities. When Jennie and John met was the sunny summer's day a military train paused in Thomasville and soldiers jumped down from one of the cars, piled into the Thomas front yard and began stripping a tree of juicy ripe cherries. Officer

RESIDENCE OF G. W. LYLES, THOMASVILLE, N. C.

The house pictured on this 1927 C. R. Thomas post card is one of several attractive residences on Thomasville's historic Salem Street. It was built in 1924 by a Mr. Wellingham for the G. W. Lyles family. Mr. Lyles was an auto agency owner in Thomasville and later in High Point. This Dutch Colonial was in the Lyles family until 1992. Owners-occupants now are Phillip Olshinski and wife Yana.

Cramer rushed up and with drawn saber and appropriate bravora chased the raiders back to the train.

One thing led to another. "Of course, I had to write a note of thanks after that," Jennie confided much later in a newspaper article she produced, "and then he must call, and kept calling, and that is the way the world goes."

Bibliography

A Hundred Years of Caring, The Story of the Baptist Children's Homes of North Carolina Inc. by Alan Keith-Lucas, 1985

Building the Back Country, An Architectural History of Davidson County by Paul Touart, 1987

Centennial History of Davidson County by J. C. Leonard, 1927

Davidson County Schools: A History 1843-1993

Files of the Mills Home Museum

Files of the North Carolina Department of Archives and History

Files of *The Thomasville Times* library

Issues of area newspapers, including *The Davidsonian, The Chairtown News, The News-Times, The Thomasville Tribune, The Thomasville Times, The* (Lexington) *Dispatch, The High Point Enterprise, and The Greensboro Daily News*

Neither Snow nor Rain, The Story of the United States Mails by Carl H. Scheele, 1970

Pathfinders Past and Present by M. Jewell Sink and Mary G. Matthews, 1972

Smithsonian Magazine (Post card article) May 1974

Stamps magazine (Post card article) February 10, 1996

The History of the Thomasville Masonic Lodge No. 214 by George M. Bailey, 1985

Thomasville City Council minutes books 1920-29

Those Millis Girls by Frances M. Bevan

Wheels of Faith and Courage by M. Jewell Sink and Mary G. Matthews, 1952

Appendix

1. Examples of personal post cards published prior to 1930.

2. Selected pages from the Thomasville Telephone Co. directory dated July 1, 1920.

80

An example of how post cards were used to preserve and circulate personal photos. The brothers pictured were prominent figures in Thomasville for many years, Robert Rapp (left), Amazon mill official, and Walter, a banker and one-time mayor. The car, a new 1920 model Grant, had been sold to them recently by Thomasville drug store owner C. R. Thomas, local Grant dealer. The Rapps posed for this photo on Highway 109 while on their way to Winston-Salem.

This post card was produced by C. W. Rochelle of High Point and is imprinted with a 1912 Thomasville post mark on its address side. It is a so-called private card sent by Mrs. J. W. Peacock to a relative in Lakeland, Fla. Apparently the children were photographed at the Peacock home on Salem Street in Thomasville and are probably the Peacock offspring, (from left) Juanita, Evelyn, James and Clarice.

Creation of a residential subdivision on the southern edge of Thomaville has begun in this 1927 C. R. Thomas post card. The billboard promotes the sale of lots and encourages prospective buyers to contact J. Walter Lambeth. In the archway, records indicate, are Lambeth himself (right), his Cadillac, and C. R. Thomas. Cedar Lodge Park was next to or a part of Cedar Lodge farm, in which Lambeth had an interest. The metal arch now is part of a gate to Mills Home.

This post card captures the entire Thomasville police force as it was constituted in 1916. Members gathered in Thomasville's Dobbson's Studio in January of that year for this portrait. Seated left is the chief, Shelby Bodenheimer. Next to him is Bruce Talbert. In back are Man Clodfelter (left), killed in the line of duty in 1920, and Albert Walker. Talbert served as chief later on.

Directory - Thomasville Telephone Co. - July 1, 1920
J.A. Green, Pres.   J.L. Sink, Supt.   J.F. Hayden, Mgr., Sec.

—A—

Adams Evans Co.	261
Alexander W H, Rt 3	925-J
Amazon Cotton Mills Office	4161
Amazon Cotton Mills	2161
Arnold J E, Trinity, N C, Rt 1	7903

—B—

Baity T O, Farm	8145
Baity Jake, Res	4091
Barringer John H, Rt 2	7145
Ball Joseph, Rt 1	918n
Ball M L, Rt 1	900m
Bank of Thomasville	13
Beck, P W, Light, N C	934y
Beck, W P, grocer	135
Beck Andrew, Rt 4	7915
Beck A H, Rt 4	933x
Beck A J, Cid, N C	929g
Beck C P, Light, N C	910g
Beck H C, Rt 4	934n
Beck H E, Lexington, N C, Rt 2	929v
Beck H W, Rt 3	925w
Beck W M, Rt. 2	900u
Beck John, Rt 4	934g
Bennett J A, Trinity, Rt 1	7930l
Berier Mathew, Rt 2	916r
Bevans, Kennels, Rt 4	933w
Bird L E, Rt 2	8924
Black B B, Rt 1	6920
Black C T, Rt 4	7906
Black H M, Cedar Lodge Farm	909h
Black D E, Rt 3	926j
Black E A, Rt 1	902h
Black G W, Rt. 4	5906
Black J W, Rt 1	902v
Black W K, Rt 3	926g
Black Y L, Lex, N C, Rt 2	934h
Black J R, Lex, N C, Rt 2	934v
Black R F, Rt 4	934j
Black J L, Rt 4	934w
Black Andrew L, Lex, N C, Rt 2	934x
Black Luther, Lex, N C, Rt 2	932u
Blair E M, res	3192
Blair J R, res	287
Bodie Rev N D, Res	298
Bodenhiemer C M, res	7122
Bodenheimer V F, Rt 1	911w
Boggs A L, res	283
Boles Rosetta, res	195
Bowers Curtis, Res	199
Bowers A H, Rt 1	919x
Bowers A L, Rt 3	919g
Bowers A N, Rt 1	926k
Bowers A S, Rt 3	926a
Bowers F S, Rt 3	921g
Bowers J O, Rt 4	3906
Bowers J W, Rt 3	919-L
Bowers P M, Rt 1	931a
Bowers R L, Rt 3	925x
Boykin Prof J E, Res	297
Boyles J W, res	136
Branson J K, res	2194
Brewer H B, res	269
Briles T M, Trinity, Rt 1	6930
Briles W C, Trinity, Rt 1	6930i
Briles Mrs N W, res	292
Brinkley J L, res	111
Bryant C L, Rt 3	932m
Bryant E L, Rt 3	93-2L
Bryant M K, Lex, N C, Rt 2	934q
Burton I Walter Jr, Rt 2	928m
Burton J W, Rt 2	908r
Burton Walter, Rt 2	908k
Burton W H, Rt 2	908n
Burton C H, Trinity, N C, Rt 1	6907
Byerly Luther, Rt 3	922r

—C—

Carolina Cafe	120
Carolina Club	153
Carolina & Yadkin River Ry, Depot	76
Carter J D, Rt 3	919h
Cecil R F, Rt 2	917m
Cedar Lodge, Rt 3	909m
Cedar Lodge Diary, Rt 3	909r
Central Motor Co	181
City Clerk's Office and Police Sta.	183
City Pressing Parlor	63
City Pumping Station	255
City Market	266
Clark L R, Res	286
Clark J G, res	132
Clinard D W, Rt 1	931m
Clinard H P, Rt 1	918m
Clinard J A, Rt 1	900r
Clinard R L, Rt 1	918k
Clinard S A, Rt 1	900g
Clinard W A, Rt 1	931x
Clinard Mrs J F, res	2197
Clinard G G, Res	305
Clinard P C, Rt 1	900v
Clodfelter I H, Lex, N C, Rt 1	929m
Clodfelter R A, Rt 3	933m
Clodfelter J E, grocer	112
Clodfelter J Ivey, Lex, N C, Rt 2	934l
Clodfelter J A, Lex N C, Rt 2	932n
Clodfelter J W, Res	4114
Cochrane G T, res	39
Cochrane G T, Insurance	51
Columbia Panel Mfg Co	85
Collett Mrs E E, res	192
Cornell D R, grocer	82
Cornelius B W, res	6102
Comstock T S, Rt 1	911y
Conrad J L, Rt 1	900x

Name	Number
Conrad W I, Rt 1	926-L
Conrad C C, Rt 1	902j
Conrad Mrs T L, res	118
Conrad D T, Rt 4	921a
Conrad E D, Rt 1	902a
Conrad J A L, Rt 1	902w
Cox C M, Res	11
Cranford O S, res	3194
Crews Dr R W, dentist	172
Crotts J H, Lex, N C, Rt 2	932a
Crotts C G, Lex, N C, Rt 2	932w
Crouse J W, Rt 4	5930l
Crouse G W, Res	314
Crowell G E, Res	160
Crutchfield Hardware Co	117
Culbreth H G, Rt 1	913k
Culler H C, Rt 2	917v
Culler J M, Rt 2	928j
Curry J G, Rt 1	926x

—D—

Name	Number
Darr C A, Rt 1	918j
Darr E L, Rt 1	900a
Darr J C, Rt 1	2920
Darr J W, Rt 1	918g
Darr S L, Rt 2	916u
Darr S M, Rt 1	918h
Darr Erastus, Rt 1	931a
Davis Raleigh, Res	4173
Davidson Wholesale Co	133
Deaton M B, grocer	3109
Dixie Cafe	135
Donell Jim, Res	2086
Dorsett Clay, Trinity, N C, Rt 1	6903
Dorsett I L, Rt 4	2901
Dorsett J G, Trinity, Rt 1	3903

—E—

Name	Number
Easter, Mrs J M, Rt 4	9912
Eddinger B M, Rt 1	925h
Eddinger D W, Rt 1	902m
Eddinger Ida, res	4199
Eddinger Henry, Rt 1	931k
Eddinger R H, Rt 1	3196
Eddinger John, Rt 1	902r
Eddinger W M, Rt 3	925a
Eddinger W H, Res	197
Elliot L W & Sons, general mdse	42
Elliott J A, Res	299
Eskridge A C, res	157
Evans G A, res	7197
Everhart F E, res	272
Everhart W H, Rt 4	932q
Everhart A S, Rt 3	925y
Everhart Felix, Rt 3	925v
Everhart G T, Rt 3	925r
Everhart H E, Rt 3	8901
Everhart J C, Rt 3	4901
Everhart J H & Bro, grocer	176
Everhart J L, Rt 3	922k
Everhart S L, Rt 1	918w
Everhart Thos E, Rt 3	922m
Everhart E T, res	3184
Everhart Machine Works	50

—F—

Name	Number
Farmers Supply Co	316
Ferguson R E, res	291
File Will, Res	252
Finch Chas F, res	131
Finch T J, Trinity, N C, Rt 1	904
Fine J E, res	194
Fine H D, Rt 3	910r
First National Bank	73
Fitzgerald W G, Rt 2	928n
Fouts A A, Farm, Rt 2	911a
Fouts W A, Cid, Rt 1	910k
Fouts A A, grocer	46
Fouts A A, res	53
Fouts Mrs Agusta, Rt 3	925m
Fouts F A, Rt 3	6901
Fouts L M, Rt 4	8915
Fouts J W, Rt 4	933-L
Fouts W T, Rt 4	921u
Fowler Jno T, res	3173
French A C, Res	2091
Freedle W D, Rt 1	913r
Freedle W D, farm, Wallburg, N C	900y
Fritts H M, Lex, N C, Rt 3	929r
Fuller A W, store, Rt 4	7923
Fuller F R, Rt 4	9923
Fuller I J, Rt 4	5923
Fuller Mrs Julia, Fullers, N C, Rt 1	7914

—G—

Name	Number
Gloff Robt, res	276
Gordon, R H, Rt 3	910q
Gordon R T, Rt 3	910n
Gordon Bert, res	102
Gray Concrete Works	165
Green J A, res	15
Green J C, res	74
Green J C, furniture and undertaker	96
Glenn Anna Panel Co	163
Goode Rev C P, Res	300
Green R S, Res	3142
Griffith C M, res	189
Griffith Zed, res	130
Grimes H A, Rt 3	921r
Grimes R M, Rt 4	5901
Grimes Luther, res	3017
Grimes T W S, Rt 4	921n
Grubb H D, Rt 4	934r
Grubb Daniel, Rt 4	933n
Grubb Thomas, Lex, N C, Rt 2	932v
Grubb C F, res	282
Grubb Ambrose, Rt 3	934k
Grubb David, Thomasville, N C, Rt 3	929l
Grubb D L, Rt 4	933k
Grubb L E, Rt 4	933u
Grubb, Oscar, Lex, N C, Rt 2	932g
Grubb S A, Rt 1	916w
Guyer W F, res	83

—H—

Name	Number
Hall J T, Rt 4	6914l
Hall T H, store	45
Hall W W, Res	4102

Name	Number
Hanes R A, Res	313
Hanes Connie, Res	2199
Hanner Z V, Res	3182
Hanner A P, Rt 3	910J
Hankins H S, Agt Standard Oil Co.	280
Harris T S, res	264
Harris T F, res	271
Harris C L, res	62
Harris M R, Rt 3	905
Harris Mrs P D, Rt 3	933g
Harris W C, res	174
Harris Bros, Merchants	169
Harris H, Res	84
Harrison E S, res	114
Harrison J H, res	3114
Harmon William, res	2182
Harville Drug Co	150
Harville R C, res	98
Harville R L, res	268
Hauss Prof J N, res	171
Hedrick John, Rt 3	925k
Hedrick J A, Rt 1	931J
Hepler C L, Lex, N C, Rt 2	929y
Hepler D H, Hannersville, N C	910-L
Hepler H C, Rt 2	2907
Hepler J A, Rt 3	932l
Hepler W L, Rt 4	6914
Helpler C E, Trinity, Rt 1	3907
Helpler E L, Res	4194
Helpler L E, Hannersville	910-L
Hiatt J F, res	2111
Hiatt A M, Rt 1	911v
Hite M B, res	188
Hillard T H, res	3199
Hilton G L, Rt 2	908k
Hilton J T, Rt 2	4924
Hilton Jno W, Rt 2	908a
Hilton L M, Rt 2	928a
Hilton R T Jr, Rt 2	917x
Hilton R T Sr, Rt 2	928k
Hilton Z E, Rt 2	916y
Hilton B G, Rt 2	916k
Hilton J C, Rt 2	916m
Hilton L H, Rt 2	916n
Hill Geore, Rt 4	4930
Hobood Dr J E, res	27
Hobgood Dr J E, office	275
Hopkins S Y, store	33
Hooper R G, res	125
Hoover D E, res	37
Hoover G M, res	36
Hoover Farm	916v
Hoover L E, Trinity, N C, Rt 1	9930
Howell C M, res	100
Hughes Mrs A W, res	71
Hughes Edward, Hannersville, N C	929k
Hughes O F, Rt 4	2915
Hughes & Peace Lumber Co	41
Hunt Albert, Hannersville, N C.	929x
Hunt J G, Rt 4	8914l
Hunt W C, Rt 3	932j
Hunter M F, Res	.302

—I—

Name	Number
Imbler Peter, Lex, N C, Rt 2	932y
Imbler A W, Rt 3	933J
Imbler R L, Rt 3	919r
Imbler Harrison, Lex, Rt 2	932z
Imbler J A, Lex, Rt 2	932x

—J—

Name	Number
Jarret E J, Rt 4	4915
Jarrett W M, Rt 3	7312
Jarrett Grocery Co	105
Jarrett W H, Res	187
Jennings T E, res	77
Jewel Cotton Mills, office	107
Johnson Archibald, res	81
Jones A E, res	146
Jones F D, res	285
Jones Dolan, res	106
Jones Allen, Trinity, N C, Rt 1	2903
Jones A C, Rt 2	911g
Julian Dr C A, res	35
Julian Dr C A, office	275

—K—

Name	Number
Kanoy A P, Rt2	918x
Kanoy J W, Rt 1	902n
Kanoy T L, Rt 1	902g
Kanoy S B, Rt 2	900-L
Kanoy S L, Res	258
Kanoy J R, Res	4145
Kearns A R, Trinity, N C, Rt 1	5930
Kearns E T, res	108
Kennedy J F, Rt 3	910l
Kennedy E D, Rt 2	917h
Kennedy D D, Rt 3	910u
Kennedy H W, Rt 3	6906
Kennedy J I, Rt 3	919n
Kennedy J M, Rt 2	928x
Kenedy J W, Rt 1	902x
Kennedy Mrs Tom, Rt 4	3923
Kennedy R E, Rt 2	928g
Kennedy W M, Rt 2	908h
Kennedy R T, Rt 2	911x
Kennedy R W, Rt 3	925u
Kennedy S B, Rt 2	911r
Kennedy E C, Res	2186
Kepley W H, Rt 1	919a
Kepley J A, Lex, Rt 2	932k
Kinley N T, Cid, Rt 1	910h
Kinley S H, Rt 3	929-L
Kinley T G, Lex, N C, Rt 2	929q
Kinley W R, Rt 3	910z
Kinney J C, res	30
Kinney W H, Res	253
Kyser H R, res	128
Kyser H R, law office	155

—L—

Name	Number
Lambeth B S, Rt 2	907
Lambeth Ben S, res	69
Lambeth J W, res	10
Lambeth R L, res	92
Lambeth F S, res	48
Lambeth Chas F, res	190

Name	Number
Lambeth J E, res	151
Lambeth D H, res	4192
Lambeth P F, Rt 3	934u
Lambeth J W, Hannersville, N C	910x
Lambeth Furniture Co	94
Lambeth E C, Res	257
Lanier B F, Cid, N C	929h
Lanier N W, Cid N C	929a
Lassiter B F, res	87
Lee J W, Rt 4	2912
Lee B F, Rt 4	4912
Lee A F, Rt 4	6912
Leonard A L, Rt 3	925g
Leonard G S, Rt 3	919y
Leonard P W, Rt 1	926r
Linberg F H, Res	256
Livengood P A, Rt 1	916x
Loflin R C, Lex, N C, Rt 2	934m
Loflin J C, R 4	3914
Loflin D R, res	2109
Loftin G C, Res	307
Lohr F L, Rt 1	926w
Lohr R H, Rt 3	926u
Long W S, Res	4142
Long, J P, Res	270
Long D A, store	24
Lopp R L, Rt 1	913v
Lyles G W, Ford Sales & Service	315

—M—

Name	Number
MacRae D C, Office	54
Manuel H T, Res	141
McLendon E F, Res	173
McGhee H L, Rt 1	916a
Mallard Robt, Rt 1	931w
Marley J R, res	152
Masonic Lodge	191
Mason P R, res	265
May J H, Rt 4	933r
May J W, Hannersville, N C	929h
May H P, Hannersville, N C	929w
Mays Market	66
Mendenhall E F, Rt 2	928u
M P Parsonaeg	168
Metters C E, Rt 4	933h
Metters J F, res	116
Millis C G, res	143
Miller J H, Res	303
Miller A S, Rt 3	910a
Miller J M, Trinity, N C	3930
Miller W B, Trinity, N C	7930
Mock Mrs Mary G, res	19
Mock Hotel	57
Moore Mrs Chas, res	31
Moore Bros, general merchants	38
Moore Bros, general merchants	8
Morris W D, Rt 1	918v
Morris A S, Rt 2	917w
Morris J A, res	21
Morris J W, Rt 1	911j
Morris Z B, Rt 2	917k
Motsinger R E, Rt 1	900w
Motsinger J C, Rt 1	900j
Motter J H, res	123

Name	Number
Mullies W E, Res	2192
Murphy H F, Rt 1	900k
Murphy J A, Rt 2	911m
Murphy M P, Rt 1	911k
Murphy R L, Rt 2	917u
Murphy R P, res	70
Murphy W A, Rt 1	916g
Murphy W T, Rt 2	917r
Myers A L, res	149
Myers J R, res	89
Myers J N, res	289
Myers A Lee, Rt 1	926n
Myers C L, Rt 3	921x
Myers D L, Rt 3	922u
Myers Dr R W, Fullers, N C, Rt 1	7914l
Myers E K, Rt 1	918u
Myers Jacob, Rt 1	919m
Myers W C, res	2102
Myers B F, Rt 3	9912l
Myers S C, Rt 2	7924
Myers J Franklin, Rt 4	933a
Myers Jesse R, Rt 3	922x
Myers John F, res	184
Myers J F, Rt 3	919j
Myers Lee, South of Town	921j
Myers Mrs Mary L, Rt 1	8196
Myers W M, Rt 1	919k
Myers J W, Light, N C	934a
Myers F H, Rt 3	922w

—N—

Name	Number
National Barber Shop	277
Newby C H, res	140
North State Veneer Co	274
Newton Rev J D, res	6145
Newton J M, Office	310

—O—

Name	Number
Orphanage, Charity and Children	32
Orphanage, M L Kesler	6
Orphanage, Infirmary Building	1
Orphanage, James R Black, res	97
Orphanage, Crutchfield B F, res	3097
Owen E E, Rt 1	913x

—P—

Name	Number
Palmer Rev J A, res	170
Peace A T, res	124
Peace W H, res	29
Pearce E C, res	3179
Peacock Dr J W, res	72
Peacock & Bowers, office	148
Pegg E A, res	90
Pennington W C, Res	304
Pennington W G, res	293
People's Bank	262
Pepper E F, res	156
Perry T G, res	113
Perryman E F, Res	4086
Perryman H E, res	154
Petree J D, res	3197
Petree I I, Rt 1	5145
Petree S Z, Rt 3	7901
Phillips Dr C H, Rt 4	6923

Name	Number
Pope R L, res	104
Primm A A, Thos-Kennels	254
Pritchard C C, res	93
Proctor Phillip, Rt 1	900h
Pike Miss Mary, res	260

—R—

Name	Number
Ranes D F, Res	251
Ragan G F, store	911n
Ragan Knitting Mills	115
Ragan A H, res	110
Ragan Mrs Mamie, res	7192
Ragan W H, Rt 2	916h
Rapp Henry, res	22
Reid H L, Res	109
Rice Lee, res	9
Ridge C E, Rt 2	7907
Ritchie R T, Res	301
Robins H M, Rt 2	928
Rothrock A F, Rt 4	4906
Rothrock M R, Rt 4	8906
Rothrock I L, Rt 3	908v
Rothrock Dr J M, res	14
Royals C N, Rt 4	4923
Royals W H, res	3091
Royals A O, Res	311
Royals Ben, res	193
Russell Mrs N L, res	2184
R & T Motor Co	4

—S—

Name	Number
Sanitary Barber Shop	250
Saintsing E W, Rt 2	917x
Saintsing G W, Rt 2	917g
Saintsing B B, Rt 2	917y
Scarlett Sam, res	284
Scotten J O, res	144
Sechrist C D, Rt 4	3901
Sechrist J F, Rt 3	925n
Shirley B F, res	3102
Shoaf E C, Res	2122
Shoaf H B, res	278
Shore R H, res	2173
Shuler C H, Rt 4	921n
Shuler C E, Rt 4	2923
Shuler F H, Rt 1	913m
Shuler L J, Rt 1	913n
Shuler L J, Rt 1	931n
Shuler J L, Rt 1	931g
Shuler John, Rt 1	913a
Sigman F E, res	52
Sink R C, West of Town	2196
Sink J L, res	139
Sink A A, Rt 1	931r
Sink C A, Rt 1	6196
Sink R H, Rt 1	913j
Sink S A, Rt 3	2906
Sink W H, Rt 1	913g
Skiles Mrs L C, res	147
Small T H, Rt 1	913w
Smith E V, Rt 4	8930
Smith, F C, Res	4168
Smith L C, Trinity, N C, Rt 1	8930l
Snider Mrs J N, Rt 1	902k
Snider B M, Hannersville, N C	910y
South Side Grocery	91
Sou Finishing Mills and Dye Plant	3141
Southern Express Office	47
Southern Ry Co, Freight Depot	25
Southern Ry Co., Passenger Depot	59
Southern Public Utilities Co	3
Southern Power Co, Sub-Station	64
Sowers C H, Rt 4	5915
Sprinkle C C, Res	295
Stadium & Cohen, Merchants	28
Standard Chair Co No 1	60
Standard Chair Co No 2	2
Star Furniture Co	134
Steed R F, Res	281
Stewart J T, Res	159
Stone B W, Res	2017
Stone C J, res	178
Stone A L, Rt 2	908x
Stone J R, Rt 2	918a
Stone M H, res	56
Stone M H, law office	78
Stone R K, Rt 2	918r
Stone R L, Rt 2	917n
Stone W H, res	198
Stout W E, Rt 3	922a
Stout W V, Rt 3	910m
Strador G M, Res	126
Strayhorn Mrs H G, res	80
Strayhorn L B, res	290
Strickland Ira, res	3111
Sullivan E H, Rt 3	922n
Swaim S A, Rt 2	2924
Sugar Jacob, Merchant	186

—T—

Name	Number
Talbert R B, res	294
Taylor R E, Res	312
Teague E E, res	3122
Teague L E, res	138
Thayer C W, Rt 4	4914l
Thayer N M, Rt 4	8923
Thayer W C, Rt 4	2930l
Thomas C R, drug store	58
Thomas C R, res	20
Thomas David, Fullers, N C, Rt 1	5914
Thomas I G, Rt 3	2914l
Thomas L E, Fullers, N C, Rt 1	5914l
Thomas M C, res	119
Thomas Sylvia, res	288
Thomasville Hosiery Mills	16
Thomasville Garage & Paint Shop	67
Thomasville Chair Co, M. Off, Plt C	40
Thomasv'l Chair Co, Ship Dpt, Plt A	99
Thomasvl Chair Co, Fac Dpt, Plt A	101
Thomasville Chair Co, Plant B	121
Thomasville Chair Co, Plant D	263
Thomasville Chair Co, Mch Shop	75
Thomasville Store Co.	44
Thomasville Boardin House	273
Thomasville Drug Co.	68
Thomasville Spoke Works	55
Thomasville Tel Co, Supply Room	0
Thomasville Tel Co, Supt Office	180

Thomasville Tel Bldg., Pay Station	23
Thomasville Bakery	34
Thomasville Bottling Works	137
Thomasville Furniture Co.	95
Thomasville Graded School	179
Thomasville Realty & Trust Co.	127
Thomasville Roller Mills	12
Thomasville Shooting Club, Lodge.	103
Thomasville Veneer & Panel Co.	162
Thompson G A, res	26
Times Printing Office	18
Tomlinson Grocery Co.	65
Tomlinson Miss Del, res	4017
Tomlinson Mrs. Mary, res	3126
Tomlinson R T, Rt 1	2145
Tomlinson T H, res	5
Tomlinson Z J, Rt 2	8907
Trotter C A, Rt 3	926m
Tutor W H, res	175
Tuttle Rev R G, res	79
Tuttle C G, Rt 3	9331
Turner J C, Rt 2	6924
Tysinger B T, Res	4109
Tysinger Lee, res	88

—U—

Underwood J L, Rt 3	3912
Underwood W H, Rt 4	8912
Underwood M F, Trinity, N C, Rt 1	4903
Uwharrie Farm, Rt 4	4914

—V—

Valentine T E, Res	2114
Varner Lee, Hannersville, N C	929j
Veach J E, Rt 2	908u
Veach J W, Rt 2	908g
Veach Z M, Rt 2	908w
Vinson B B, res	167
Vinson B B, law office	7

—W—

Wagstaff O L, res	164
Wagner W J, Rt 1	931v
Wagner B B, Stable	259
Walker W R, Trinity, N C, Rt 1	2930
Walker James, Trinity, N C, Rt 1	49301
Ward Co, Mill, Rt 1	919w
Warner Herbert, Rt 3	59121
Warner Vance, res	3168
Watford A E, Light N C	6915
Watford S C, Light, N C	3915
Webb E L, res	166
Welch Ada C, res	4184
Welborn C S, Rt 3	910w
Welborn E S, Rt 1	911u
Wells Rev P I, West of Town	7196
West End Store Co.	49
West End Pressing Club	296
Western Union Telegraph Co.	43
White C L, Res	308
White J G, Trinity, Rt 1	39301
Williams Chas, Res	86
Wood W S, Rt 2	908m
Wright J D, Cid N C	929u
Wright J P, Fullers, Rt 1	5914i
Wright J D, Res	309

—Y—

Yonts M O, Rt 1	926h
Yonts Loyd, Res	267
Yow C J, Rt 4	9906
Yow G H, Res	61

—Z—

Zimmerman R E, Office	129

Index

Allen, Johnny 43
Amazon mill 5, 37, 80
Ambulance 55
Anti-Saloon League 43
"Arlam" 71
Armfield, J. L. 66
Atwater-Kent 25

B

Bandstand 63
Bank of Thomas. 8, 61
Bapt. Children's Hmes 41
Baraca class 52
Barbershop, Sanitary 63
Barnstorming 15
Baseball 9
Baywood Hotel 69
Bevan boys 63
Bevan, Frances 25
Bevan, Fred 63
Biddles, the 45
Big Chair VIII, 3, 18
Black, Fred 31
Bodenheimer, Shelby 83
Bond issue 10, 54
Boston Store 96
Bowling alley 63
Boyd, Waldo S. 15, 17
Boyles, J. W., 3, 66
Boy Scouting 71
Bride's Pride Flour 63
Brokaw Castle 35
Brooklyn Dodgers 43
Brooks, R. G., 5 & 25¢ Store 4
Burgin Co. 14
Burma-Shave sign 67
Burrus, Dr. J. T. 55
Byerly Graded School 60

C

Caskets 65
Carolina Underw. Co. 5
Cates Block 14
Cates Building 63
Cedar Ldge Farm 45, 82

Cedar Ldge Park 82
Cemetery Assn. of Thomasville 33
Cemetery, City 31, 33
Central Motor Co. 63
"Chair City" slogan 3
Chairtown News, The VI, 49
"Chairtown of the South" 3
Chevrolets 63
Chiropractor 63
Chrysanthemum show 69
City Council, Thom. 15
City Hall 33, 36, 51, 61
City manager form 3
Civic Center 73, 95
Civic Improvement League 29, 35
Cleveland Indians 43
Clinic, city 55
Clodfelter, Man 19, 83
Coca-Colas 3
Colgates, the 45
Collier's magazine 65
Colonial Drive 21
Colonial Dr. Elem. Sch. 58
Community Meth. Church 50, 71, 73, 95
Conrad Hill Township 21
Cooksey, R. M. 33
Courtroom, city 51, 53
Cove Glen, N. C. 43
Cramer Furn. Co. 30, 32
Cramer, John T. 30, 75, 77
Crutchfield Hdwe 14, 53
"Crutchfield Jail" 51

D

Davidson Academy 60
Davidsonian, The 49
Deltiology V
Dempsey, Jack 13
Denton 59
Depot, freight 4, 26
Depot, Thomasville 4, 22, 24, 45, 59
Dewey, Mr. and Mrs. 69
Dispatch, The V, 37
Dobbson's Studio 83
Drummond's Pictorial Atlas 5
Duke Power 29

E

East Davidson Sch. 60
Eldridge, Rube 9, 11
Electric lights 29
Eller, C. B. 11
Elliott, Austin 51
Ellison, J. C. 63
Everhart's Dairy 65
Everybody's Day 35, 38

F

Fair Grove Consolidated
  School 60
Fast, Dr. Walter L. 63
Fife, Eugenia 65
Finch Block 51, 53
Finch
  Brown 57, 59
  Charles F. 5, 27, 49,
    51, 71, 73, 95
  Mrs. Charles F. 71, 95
  Doak 57, 73
  Ernestine 68
  George 57, 73
  T. Austin 37, 68, 73
  T. J. 57, 73
  T. J., sons 73
Firemen, volunteer 53
Fire department, city 74
Fire station, city 51, 53
Fire truck, city 23, 53, 55
Firpo, Luis 13
First Baptist Church 48
First Meth. Protestant
  Church 71
First Nat'l Bank 36, 61, 74
First Nat'l Bank Bldg. 36,
  55, 61
Fleer, Alice 47
Fleer, Frank H. 45, 47
Football 11
Ford truck 53
Fritts, Earl 25
Fuller Brush 65
Fuller's Mill 72

G

Gardner, Rev. E. Norfleet 43
German Luger 17

Glen Anna Fem. Sem. 40
Glen Anna Plantation 59
Goulds, the 45
Grace Lutheran Church 13
Grand Rapids, Mich 3
Grange, Red 13
Gray, Mary 40
Green, J. A. 84
Green, J. C. 31, 65
Green, J. C., funeral hme 55
Green, Rev. Jim 41
Greensboro High School 35
Gymnasium 71

H

Haldeman, G. W. 15, 17
Harris, C. J. 51
Harris, C. L. 2
Harville Drug Store 16
Hauss, J. N. 23
Hayden, J. F. 84
Hearse 55
Hiatt, A. Mack 49
High Point, Thomasville
  & Denton RR 59
Hinkle Milling 63
Hinkle, William 71
Hogeye 71
Hog Lot 29
Hooker, Grady 29
Hose, handreels of 53
Hospital, City Mem. 57, 62
Hospital, Comm. Gen'l 62
Hundley, George L. 23, 61

I

Influenza epidemic 19, 21
Indoor plumbing 29

J

Jail, city 51, 53
Jenkins, L. C. 19
Jennings, Dr. R. G. 55, 57
Jewel mill 5
Jewel Tea 65
Johnson, Archibald 49
Johnson, Gerld 21, 39, 49
Jones, Bobby 13
Jones's Dairy 65
Jones, Capt. Milton 59, 61
Julian, Dr. C. A. 39, 96

K

KDKA 25
Kaiser Bill 47
Kelvinator 65
Ku Klux Klan 67
Kyser, Howell 25
Kyser, Kay 25, 27

L

Lambeth Bldg 6, 12, 16
Lambeth, John, Bldg 16
Lambeth
  Charles F. 69
  Ernestine 68, 75
  Frank S. 37, 49, 69, 71
  James E. 69
  John W. 49, 75
  J. Walter 49, 82
  R. L. 39
Lambeth's Dairy 65
Lee Amusement Co. 25
Lee, R. C. 63
Lee, R. C., Riding
  Devices 63
Liberty magazine 65
Library, public 37, 51, 73, 95
Lindbergh, Charles A. 13
"Lone Eagle," The 15
Lufsey, Virginia 15
Lyles Ford Agency 63
Lyles, G. W. 41, 76
Lyles, G. W., residence 76

Mc

McMcIntyre, Mrs. W. H. 20

M

Madeleine 39
Main St. Meth. Ch. 11, 41,
  50, 52, 61, 69, 71, 73
Main Street School 54, 56
Manassa Mauler 13
Masons 33
Masonic lodge 33
Memorial Meth.
  Church 50, 52, 73
Millis boarding house 63
Millis, Frances 63
Mills Home 41, 82
Mills, J. H. 43
Mock, John A. 69
Mock, Mrs. John A. 20
Mock Hotel 4, 20, 22, 37, 67
Model-T 25
Monkey Hollow 39
Montgomery County 59
Morris, J. M., &
  Sons IV, V, 38

N

Nat'l Gallery of Art 39
National Highway 39
News, The 49
News-Times, The 51
New York Giants 43
Norfolk Southern RR 1
N. C. Railroad 1
N. C. Smelting Wrks 69
North State Tel. Co. 47

O

Olshinski, Phillip 76
Olshinski, Yana 76
Onion Hill 39
Opera House 21, 27

P

Page Trust 34, 61
Palace Theater 27, 43
"Paradise Hill" 41
Parham, B. W. 49
Passenger depot 4,
  22, 24, 45, 59
Patterson, Rev. Charlie 13
Peacock
  Clarice 21, 81
  Evelyn 21, 81
  Dr. J. W. VI, 15, 17,
    31, 41, 47, 53, 55
  Mrs. J. W. 13, 81
  James 81
  Juanita 81
Peacock, Dr. J. W., res. 70
Peoples Bldg & Loan 74
Pennington, W. Casper 5
Phi Beta Club 31
Phillips, Dr. C. H. 55, 72
Phillips, Vera Green 47
Police station, city 51
Pope, R. L. 27, 70
Pope, R. L., Bible Cl. 52
Post office 14, 28, 51, 66
Primm, Archie 2, 45

Primm, Ruth 63
Prohibition 17
Pullman cars 45

R

Rabbit Quarter 39
Ragan, A. Homer 49, 74
Ragan Knitting 5, 40, 74
Rapp, Mrs. Henry 69
Rapp, Robert 37, 80
Rapp, Walter W. 80
Reddick, T, L. (Lev) 19
Reo auto 59
Restrooms, public 51
Rich Fork Bapt. Church 43
Ritchie, M. L. 66
Rochelle, C. W. 81
Rockefellers, the 45
Roosevelt, Franklin D. 49
Rotary club 37
Rounsaville, Dr. Henry 75
Rural Free Delivery IV
Ruth, Babe 13

S

Salem Street 10, 39
Salisbury High School 35
Sanitary Barbershop 63
Sanitary Lunch 63
Sanitary Pressing Club 63
*Saturday Evening
   Post* magazine 65
Schadt, Everett W. 29
Sears & Roebuck 25
Sechriest, John F. 33
Sewer system 29
Sheik," "The 27
Shore, Paul 49
"Shouting Methodists" 39
Sidewalks 63
Sink, J. L. 84
Sirens 55
Skiles Heights 72
Slimey Corner 39
Southern Public Util. 29
South. RR 1, 57, 59, 67, 96
Sou. RR depot 4, 22, 24,
   45, 59, 67
Southside Dairy 65
"Spirit of St. Louis" 13
Stanback Headache
   Powders 7
Stanback, Thomas J. 7

Std Chair Co. 53, 55, 69
State Industrial Bank 61
State Commercial Bank 12
Still, liquor 19
Street-paving 10, 63
Sunnyside Dairy 65

T

Talbert, Bruce 83
Taylor, J. E. 17, 19, 41, 53
Tennessee Jazz Orch. 67
Tennis 11
Thomas, C. R., Block 8
Thomas
   Charles R. IV, V, VI, 2,
      7, 9, 37, 64, 80, 82
   Drug Store V, 7, 16
   Jennie 75, 77
   John W. V, 7, 33, 45,
      64, 69, 75
   Mary Lambeth 75
   Ped 45
   Dr. R. W. 64
Thomas, Jn W., res. 6, 18, 64
Thomasville
   and Glen Anna RR 59
   Bapt. Orphanage V, VI, 41,
      42, 43, 44, 46
   Bottling Works 3
   Chamber of Commerce 96
   Chair Co. 5, 30, 32, 73
   Chair Factory 1
   Depot 4, 22, 24, 45, 59
   Drug Store 6, 12, 53
   Family Laundry 5
   Female College 40
   Furniture Industries 32. 75
   Graded School 21, 54, 56
   High School 56
   Hosiery Mills 5
   Public Library 73
   Rotary Club 37
   Shooting Club 2, 41, 45
   Store Co. 65
   Telephone Co. 47
   Woman's Club 31, 75
   Times, The 51
   *Thomasville,Chairtown
      of the South* 96
Three-Hat Mountain 47
Tilden, Bill 13
Times, The 49, 51
Tourist court 67
Tuttle, Rev. R. G. 41

U

Underpass 57
University of N. C. 25
U. S. Ambassador
  to Austria 49

V

Valentino, Rudolph 25
Veach, Wesley 45

W

Waddell, Mrs. Evelyn 70
Wagoner, Minnie 69
Wagner, Brack 61
Walker, Albert 83
Walker, Dr. Nat 72
Walker, Pauline 72
Waterworks 29
Webb, Cecil VI
Webb, E. L. 11
Webb, Eugene 11
Wellingham, Mr. 76
Wesley Mem. Meth. Ch. 17
Western Union Telegraph 47
Westmoreland, D. S. 1, 3, 49
Westmoreland, J. F. 49
Westmoreland Hill 49
Whistles, factory 53, 55
Willowmoore Springs 67
Wildcat", "The, whistle 53
Work & Win Club 35
World Series 43
World War I 19, 29, 45, 51
World War II 49

X-Y-Z

X-ray 55
Yokeley, Dr. R. V. 35, 55
Yow, George 63

95

Location of the building on this post card was in the first block of Randolph Street, now that of the Thomasville Public Library. It was built in 1923 by Charles F. Finch as a memorial to his wife and to serve as the Community Methodist Church. The photo here was made after the building, appearing the same as when first opened, became the city-owned Civic Center in 1952. It burned in 1976. Attempts to find a card showing the church in the 20s failed.

Rather than taken from a post card, this photograph of the elegant Dr. C. A. Julian residence in Thomasville is shown as it appears in a publication entitled *Thomasville, Chair Town of the South* that was published around 1916, probably by the first Thomasville Chamber of Commerce. The house stood on East Main Street looking out on the Southern Railway. Its location was about the same as the Boston Store's today. Dr. Julian was a beloved physician for many years. When no longer his home, the house was put to various uses. It burned down during the early 1940s.